OREGON TIMES AND TRAILS

by Joan and Gene Olson

"The men of our Pacific Northwest are a noble lot of freemen. The spirit of enterprise which led them across the untracked continent to form a new empire, beside our sundown sea, was a bold and free spirit; and the patient heroism of the few women who originally shared their lot had in it the elements of grandeur."

-- *Abigail Scott Duniway*

WINDYRIDGE PRESS

Book design by Carl Thomas
Cover photo: Denver Public Library Western Collection
Additional Photos: Culver Pictures, Inc., 6 & 7
Oregon State Highway Department, 45, 95, 97, 98, 123, 168, 169, 182, 185, 188, 189
Author, 77
Harvey Dickey, 79
The Oregonian, 118
Vasey-SP&S Railway, 130, 133, 136
Oregon State Forestry Department, 143, 149, 151, 153, 161
Eyerly Aircraft — Oregon State Forestry Department, 145
Oregon State University Extension Service, 150
Ackroyd-Port of Portland, 171, 176, 177, 181
Port of Portland, 175
All other photos: Oregon Historical Society

Revised second printing 1972

Library of Congress Catalog Card Number: 65 - 23503

PUBLISHED BY WINDYRIDGE PRESS, 780 OXYOKE ROAD,
GRANTS PASS, OREGON

PRINTED IN THE UNITED STATES OF AMERICA

TABLE OF CONTENTS

ACKNOWLEDGMENTS

The gratitude of the authors must go first to Walter Foelker, social studies chairman at Hillsboro Union High School, then to W. Ray Carder, curriculum director in the same district. These two were indispensable. Without their inspiration, advice and encouragement at many points along a hard road, there would have been no "Oregon Times and Trails."

Special thanks, too, must go to Ethel Jensen and Harriet Lehman, eighth grade core teachers at Hillsboro, who have been involved fruitfully in the project since the beginning, and to the many eighth graders at Hillsboro who tested the book and convinced us that we were moving in the right direction.

Anyone who sets out to amass material for a work of this kind must seek in many places. In some of those places, he finds exceptionally helpful and perceptive persons. In this category, we will remember Mrs. Barbara Elkins, Oregon Historical Society; Lee Harter, Office of State Forester; the staff of the Josephine County Library, particularly Mrs. Bennett Hill; and E. A. Miller, The Port of Portland.

Others who contributed materially are Lloydene Hurt Barbour; Supt. Tom Calkins, Josephine County Unit; Harvey Dickey; R. S. Duter, U. S. Bureau of Public Roads; Victor Freyer, Oregon State Highway Dept.; Earl R. Gillis, Newberg Public Schools; Jean Hallaux, Astoria Chamber of Commerce; Marvin Harrold; Ross and Alice Huntsinger; Margaret Knispel, Beaverton Public Schools; W. Verne McKinney, Hillsboro "Argus"; John James Murray; Arthur V. Myers, Salem Public Schools; Mrs. Albert H. Powers, Oregon Landmarks Committee; Charles R. Ross, Oregon State University Extension Service; Mel, Lorena and Bill Sample; Hal W. Schiltz, Myrtle Creek "Mail"; Dr. B. L. Simmons, Oregon State Department of Education; Ronald O. Smith, Portland Public Schools; Carl and Leona Thomas; Alex Troffey, Kaiser Industries; Vern Vasey, Spokane, Portland & Seattle Railway; Albert Wiesendanger, Keep Oregon Green Association.

Thank you all.

Joan and Gene Olson
Grants Pass, Oregon

AUTHORS' NOTE

Books for suggested reading at the end of each chapter are specifically selected for junior high school readers. Unfortunately, little has been published for young readers in some subject areas.

The selected bibliography at book's end is made up largely of adult books but many will provide good supplemental reading where additional material is needed.

CHAPTER ONE – The Explorers:

INTO THE SHINING MOUNTAINS

The slim young man faced his partner in command and muttered, "Horses, Billy, got to have horses. If we don't get them, they'll be finding our bones in these mountains."

Lieutenant William Clark, weak from an infection but still the lighthearted optimist, slapped the buckskin sleeve of Captain Meriwether Lewis and tried to smile. "Maybe ... maybe. But the Shoshone have all the horses we need, remember. Just —"

"Shoshone!" raged Captain Lewis, smashing his fist against his thigh. "Where are they? Maybe they don't exist at all! Have you thought of that?"

Clark turned his head slowly to glance at the young Indian woman who was rubbing the feet of her husband, Toussaint Charbonneau, who sat on the bank of the rushing stream near which the exploring party had camped.

"Janey exists," said Clark softly, using his nickname for Sacajawea, the Shoshone woman who had joined their group many months ago with her husband. "Janey is Shoshone. The Shoshone exist. We'll find them, my friend."

Lewis, an intense, brooding man, stared at his ailing partner for a moment, then managed a thin smile. "Not quite right, Billy. Not 'we.' You'll have to wait until you get well. I'll leave in the morning with Drouilliard, Shields and ... McNeal, I think. We'll find Shoshones and we'll get horses. We'll come back with horses ... or we won't come back at all."

Night settled into the river encampment. Captain Lewis wrapped himself in his blankets on the unyielding ground. For a long time he was unable to sleep. He turned to stare westward

1

The Lewis a

ark Expedition

at the Shining Mountains as the last light touched their fearsome, snow-capped peaks. Although the day had been brutally hot, already the chill of night was creeping in; summer was waning. Lewis knew that those terrible mountains would soon be caught in the icy grip of winter. The peaks had to be conquered within a month ... or they would not be conquered at all. They must be conquered on horses ... or they would not be conquered at all.

And only the Shoshone, the legendary tribe which supposedly lived in the Shining Mountains, could supply the horses.

Lewis knew that if his mission failed, most of his gallant men would surely die. This prospect was not the worst one, though; these men had accepted the possibility of death when they left St. Louis many months before.

But what of President Thomas Jefferson in far-off Washington? He had chosen Lewis to lead this expedition because in the president's mind was a grand design — a United States of America which stretched from ocean to ocean, from the Atlantic to the Pacific. If the expedition failed, or arrived too late at the mouth of the fabled great River of the West, the vast, unexplored land west of the Rocky Mountains might be claimed by Great Britain and would be forever British, not American.

Troubled, anxious to face the threat and promise of tomorrow, Captain Meriwether Lewis fell into fitful sleep.

On the bank of the Jefferson River, a thousand miles west of civilized America, a loon stirred in the night and sent forth its eerie cry.

* * * * *

The Lewis and Clark expedition had boarded a keel boat at St. Louis on May 14, 1804, and had begun to pole against the current of the mighty Missouri River.

The regular party totalled thirty-two men when the boats shoved off from St. Louis. One of the most famous members of the expedition, Sacajawea, was to join later with her husband, the clumsy, cowardly Charbonneau. Soon after joining, 17-year-old Sacajawea provided a most interesting addition to the party by giving birth to a son, called "Baptiste" by his father, but quickly nicknamed "Pompey" by the merry Clark.

When first approached by Charbonneau, Lewis had been reluctant to take him along, even though the party needed an

4

interpreter who understood the language of the plains Indians.

"I suppose you would want to take your wives along," Lewis said. "No white man has ever been where we are going. No woman could stand the trip."

"I would take Sacajawea only," bargained Charbonneau. "Her back is strong. She carries like a man. She is not a Minnetaree, even though we have lived with that tribe for years. She is a Shoshone. I swear in my heart that she is a Shoshone, stolen as a young girl by Minnetarees and sold as a slave."

"Shoshone" seemed to be the magic word; at any rate, Lewis agreed to take Charbonneau and his Indian wife along.

Charbonneau was not the only man of French blood who joined. Among the others was George Drouilliard, who knew Indian sign language.

There were several in the party of more than ordinary interest. There was Peter Cruzatte, for instance, who took his violin along and played for dancing on festive occasions all the way across the continent.

There was York, Clark's servant and the only Negro in the group. York proved strong and faithful and was a constant source of amazement to Indians encountered along the way. Never having seen a man with black skin before, they persisted in wetting their fingers and rubbing York, expecting the dark paint to rub off. York endured this patiently; in fact, he was often amused. Once, though, York's color wasn't funny at all. The party encountered Selish Indians, to whom black was the color of war paint. In order to quiet the suddenly angry Indians, it was necessary for York to submit again to the wet finger test.

There was also Private George Shannon, the youngest member of the expedition. Little more than a boy, Shannon developed an annoying habit of getting lost. The first time it happened, he almost starved before he found his way back to the expedition.

Perhaps the most unusual member of the party was a Newfoundland dog, Scannon. Captain Lewis had bought him for twenty dollars, a very high price in those times, but the dog paid his way by catching game and returning with it to his master.

This strange group had endured much in fighting its way up the Missouri to within sight of the Shining Mountains — sickness, many tense moments with irritable and savage Indians, rattlesnake

5

Mandans in

ting York

invasions so terrible that some of the men insisted on sleeping in the boats and finally, grizzly bears weighing half a ton which outran horses and shrugged off bullets from the punchless rifles of the day like buffalos flicking away flies.

But they had survived these hazards, and mutiny as well, only to face the threat of failure many hundreds of hard miles from St. Louis. They had exchanged their keel boats for canoes. Finally the canoes became useless in the shallow, rocky tributaries of the Missouri along which they had to pass on their way westward. With members of the party weak from illness, with heavy supplies to carry, they could not cross the Shining Mountains on foot fast enough to escape the onrushing winter.

It was then, with the rough mountains looming ahead and winter little more than a calendar page away, that the horses became a matter of success or failure, life or death...

* * * * *

"Look, George!" cried Captain Lewis as he bent over the faint trail which led toward the mountains.

The Frenchman trotted over quickly, squatted and put his finger into a ghostly track in the dust. He lifted his head and smiled.

"Shoshone," murmured Drouilliard.

"With horses," added Lewis. "Horses, George!"

The others wanted to push on quickly along the trail but Lewis ordered Drouilliard to return to a stream fork which they had recently passed in order to leave a message for Clark and the main body of the expedition. Lewis hoped that Clark would soon recover sufficiently from his illness to travel at least as far as the fork.

While Drouilliard was gone, Captain Lewis planned his advance. He knew that his little group faced two dangers, one almost as terrible as the other. First, the Shoshones might consider them enemies and kill them all. Second, the Shoshones might fear them enough to hide and never appear.

In either case, there would be no Shoshone ponies to carry the Lewis and Clark expedition over the Shining Mountains.

Captain Lewis sent Drouilliard far out on the left flank and Shields to the other. Captain Lewis and McNeal would cover the center. It was decided that the first man to discover a Shoshone trace would raise his rifle with his hat upon it. This was to avoid a noise that would alarm the Indians.

The slow advance began. For a time that seemed endless, they saw nothing.

Then Captain Lewis snatched at his telescope and trained it toward a pass which cut through the hills ahead.

He made out plainly a mounted Indian riding toward them!

Apparently the Indian didn't know they were there. Lewis's heart leaped when he could not recognize the Indian's garments. This was a strange tribe. This might be a Shoshone, at last!

Lewis hastily signalled by putting his hat on his rifle, then motioned Drouilliard to close in.

Finally, as he reached a point about a mile away, the Indian saw the tense Lewis and pulled up his mount.

Quickly Lewis grabbed a blanket and spread it on the ground in the traditional gesture of friendship.

The Indian didn't move.

Twice more Lewis made the sign. Again it failed to make an impression on the Indian.

Then Drouilliard and Shields came into view and the Indian started away in fright.

Pulling some trinkets out of his bag, Lewis started slowly forward. The Indian stopped and watched suspiciously.

His scalp prickling with tension, Lewis edged forward, putting one foot carefully ahead of another in the manner of a man afraid of quicksand.

Then, when Lewis was only a few hundred feet away, the Indian wheeled his mount and started to gallop away.

Lewis despairingly cried out a Shoshone word supposedly meaning "white man" which he had been taught by Sacajawea.

"Ta-ba-bo-ne! Ta-ba-bo-ne!"

Lewis signalled his men to halt. Everyone stopped except Shields, who hadn't caught the signal. The Indian watched Shields closely. Lewis took the opportunity to advance still farther, pulling up his sleeve to show his white forearm, wanting desperately to make it plain that they were not Minnetarees, traditional enemies of the Shoshones.

Then came heartbreak as the Indian whirled, whipped his horse and disappeared into the brush.

Crushed by disappointment, Lewis slumped to the ground. He knew that the lone rider would warn the Shoshone camp. Now it was more important than ever that Lewis and his men act as friendly as possible.

Drouilliard squatted nearby. "We rest now, Captain?"

Lewis drew himself up. "We'll build a fire and cook, George. That might convince them we mean no harm."

But no more Shoshones appeared.

*****

When they departed from the campsite, they left gifts as a further guarantee of their good intentions. And now Lewis broke out his American flag and carried it in plain view.

For several days, they saw no Shoshones, but they still found tracks. Then they saw two squaws and a warrior, but the Indians fled before any friendly sign could be made.

Again, Lewis could only swallow his disappointment and order his men forward along the trail.

Suddenly their opportunity struck. As they walked around a blind corner in a ravine, they almost stumbled over an old Indian squaw, a young squaw and a very young girl.

The young woman wailed and fled in fear up the ravine.

The old woman and the girl seemed to realize immediately that they had no chance to escape. As Lewis neared, they lowered their heads to expose their necks to the expected tomahawk.

"Ta-ba-bo-ne," said Lewis softly, although he was beginning to wonder by this time if Sacajawea had given him the right word. (Perhaps she hadn't; the word may have been understood as "stranger" by the Shoshones.)

Then Lewis showed her the white skin on his forearm and offered presents.

"George," said Lewis gently, "tell her we mean no harm. Ask her to call back the young squaw."

The Frenchman nodded and spoke in sign language. The old woman frowned as she tried to understand. Then the fear left her eyes and she cried out in Shoshone. Soon the young woman

10

reappeared and accepted with pleasure the gifts of mirrors and moccasins and beads.

"Now ask them to take us to their camp," instructed Lewis.

Drouilliard nodded again and began to speak with his hands.

The women consulted in Shoshone. Then the young one helped the old woman to her feet. The young woman picked up the girl and started off, beckoning at Lewis.

They had gone but a few miles when they met a Shoshone party of sixty warriors, on its way to fight off what they thought was an attack by Minnetarees.

Feeling that the women had led him into a trap, Lewis immediately dropped his rifle, raised the flag high and moved forward alone. The captain felt sweat roll down his face as he fought to keep his eyes fixed on the nearest warriors, whose stern faces promised only death. Lewis knew that if he displayed any sign of weakness or fear in this crucial moment, there were only seconds of life left to him and there would be no Shoshone ponies to ride over the Shining Mountains. But he knew also that if he appeared angry or threatening, he would die as quickly.

Advancing slowly, he breathed just a little easier when he saw confusion on the faces of the nearest warriors. Confusion bought a little time; now just a few more desperate minutes might save his life and bring success to his mission.

Now a few Shoshones began to ask anxious questions of the handsome warrior who seemed to be their chief. Lewis could not understand the nervous voices but he could guess what the questions were:

What was this tall, strange-looking man? Why was he carrying that peculiar banner? Was he friend or foe?

Before these questions could be answered with a Shoshone arrow unleashed toward the heart of Lewis, the three women, laden with their gifts and obviously unharmed, came into view!

Lewis felt sharp surprise as the warriors leaped down off their horses and embraced him and his men, smearing their cheeks with war paint.

A council was arranged on the spot and peace pipes were smoked.

The Shoshone chief, Cam-me-ah-wait, accepted the American

Lewis and Clark medallion

flag. More discussions were held. It was agreed that the Shoshones would take horses and would return to the stream fork with Lewis for a meeting with Clark and the main body.

It developed that the Shoshones were near starvation. When Drouilliard responded by going on a hunt and shooting three deer, the Shoshones were almost beside themselves with gratitude and chewed hungrily on the fresh meat while casting appreciative glances at their powerful white friends.

When they approached the Clark camp, Sacajawea went into a joyful dance, then ran to Cam-me-ah-wait and embraced him with great happiness.

The Shoshone chief was her brother, whom she had not seen since she had been kidnapped by the Minnetarees more than ten years before!

Watching the display of affection with a broad smile, William Clark approached Captain Lewis. "You never do things by halves, do you, Meriwether? Horses for us and a brother for Janey. By the way, Captain, what would they say in Washington if they knew you'd taken to painting your face?"

The solemn Lewis brushed at his cheek, stared in surprise at his painted fingertips, then smiled wearily.

"I've always found it easy to make friends, Billy. You know that."

THE BACKGROUND

History, marching down the years, has a way of leaving footprints.

Passing time and the clotting of population erase many of them; then only words in books mark trails for new generations.

Man can imagine that old life when he reads about it; he can almost touch it when he sees the marks the old ones left. Oregonians are fortunate in this respect. Great expanses of Oregon and the Pacific Northwest look much as they did long ago. The wilderness rivers reaching toward the sea and the soaring stands of timber in the far-back country have changed little from the days when Lewis and Clark first ventured through on their journey to that legendary ocean called Pacific.

* * * * *

The Lewis and Clark party, riding Shoshone ponies and with an old Shoshone brave as guide, came down off the Lolo Trail, then struck out on the fabled river of the West, the Columbia, in Indian canoes. The explorers, with great rejoicing, reached the Pacific Ocean at the mouth of the Columbia in November, 1805.

They chose a spot about seven miles south of Astoria for their winter headquarters; a fort was built. This place became known as Fort Clatsop; it bears this name today. The fort has been restored and was designated a National Memorial in 1958. It is the outstanding landmark of the Lewis and Clark Expedition in Oregon.

Near the south end of the promenade at Seaside is another memento of the journey, a cairn marking the place where party members boiled ocean water in large kettles to get salt for the enlivening of their meals, which consisted during that winter mainly of elk meat and roots.

Not surprisingly, rain tormented the exploring party during their winter sojourn at Ft. Clatsop, as did too-friendly Clatsop Indians. In March of 1806, the party broke camp for the return journey and reached St. Louis in September of the same year.

Upon arrival, Captain Lewis scrawled a quick summary to be sent to President Thomas Jefferson:

"In obedience to your orders we have penetrated the Continent of North America to the Pacific Ocean and sufficiently explored the interior of the country to affirm that we have discovered the most practicable communication which does exist across the continent."

Thus ended one of the most difficult and important journeys of exploration ever attempted. Now Americans understood for the first time what a strange and wonderful land President Jefferson had acquired for the United States when he made the Louisiana Purchase.

In addition to other rewards, Lewis was appointed governor of the vast Louisiana Territory. But his career had passed its high point; as governor, his troubles mounted. When Jefferson went out of office, Lewis lost his friend at court, and fell into further difficulty. A solitary man who was most comfortable in the wilds, Meriwether Lewis made a poor adjustment to the life of a politician.

Finally, Lewis started a political fencemending trip to Washington, D. C., along the infamous Natchez Trace, which was known to be patrolled by cutthroats of all descriptions.

It was at Grinder's Stand along the Natchez Trace that Meriwether Lewis, 35 years old, was shot through the head on the night of October 10, 1809. Mystery still surrounds his death. The Grinders, who had taken him in for the night, called it suicide. There are others who say he was murdered for the money he carried.

In either event, it was a poor end for a great man.

William Clark fared much better. He occupied himself with much gusto and popularity as a brigadier general in charge of

Fort Clatsop reconstructed

Indian affairs for Louisiana Territory, then was named governor of Missouri Territory. He died in 1838.

They died, along with Sacajawea, York, and the rest, but Oregonians will never forget that they lived.

SUGGESTED READING

Bakeless, John Edwin; THE ADVENTURES OF LEWIS AND CLARK; Houghton Mifflin; 1962.

Dryden, Cecil Pearl; BY SEA ON THE TONQUIN; Caxton; 1956.

Farnsworth, Frances Joyce; WINGED MOCCASINS, THE STORY OF SACAJAWEA; Messner; 1954.

Parrish, Philip H.; BEFORE THE COVERED WAGON; Binfords & Mort; 1931.

Powers, Alfred; TRUE ADVENTURES ON WESTWARD TRAILS; Little Brown; 1954.

Salisbury, Albert and Jane; TWO CAPTAINS WEST Superior; 1950.

CHAPTER TWO – Early Government:
TALKER OF THE TERRITORY

There was a man who talked his way into Oregon history.

This is not exaggeration; this is historical fact. If this man had not been such a talker, Oregon today might be a province of Canada.

The man's name was Joseph L. Meek. There was nothing "meek" about him. If the Indians had given him a name, it would certainly have been something like "Big Chief Loose Tongue of the Largemouth Tribe." His nickname would have been "Flapjaw."

They said that Joe Meek could talk the bark off a tree. They said that when Joe began to talk, the squirrels dropped their acorns and sat on a limb to listen. They said that the lovely song of the Oregon surf off Rockaway Beach had no more music than a rusty saw blade compared to Joe Meek in full cry as he talked a homesteader out of his last haunch of venison toward the end of a hard winter.

He may well have been Oregon's first and best confidence man. He rode his mouth cross-country in 1847-48. He had been granted expense money but, in his characteristic way, he had spent it in celebration with his friends. He had lots of friends. But he was due in Washington, D. C., three thousand miles away, to plead the cause of territorial government of Oregon.

You didn't cross the North American continent in midwinter in those days unless you were insane ... or unless you were Joe Meek.

Joe Meek reached Washington. Of course, he did. Without expense money, he talked his way cross-country.

17

His adventures along the way deserve a book of their own. His crashing impact on Washington society deserves another.

Picture a bearded, dirty, leather-clad character from the wilds of Oregon descending upon the sophisticated East to tell outrageous stories, some of them true, about the wild life he had lived ...

"Aren't you worried," one plump, bejeweled matron asked him, "about leaving your wife alone among all those savage Indians?"

"Shucks, no!" boomed Meek. "My wife IS an Indian!"

This, at least, was pure truth. All of Joe's wives had been Indians, the first a member of the Snake tribe, the other two Nez Perces.

Certainly the Washington matron dropped her lorgnette. Joe Meek had a way of striking people like a fir log borne on a Willamette River flood crest.

But the story of Joe Meek didn't begin in Washington, D. C. Let's go back a few years ...

* * * * *

He came out of the mountains, Joe Meek did, in 1840, when the fur trade died. He left legendary friends of the fur trade days like Sublette and Bridger and Kit Carson and joined another fur trader, his brother-in-law Robert Newell, in a trek to the Willamette Valley.

He took up a homestead four miles north of what is now Hillsboro in the fertile, rain-washed Tualatin Valley.

Meek wasn't cut out to be a homesteader. He had an inbred dislike of dull chores, for one thing. He realized early on that it was much simpler to talk one's way into a square meal than to grow it.

So Joe circulated. He enlivened many a homesteader's evening with colorful tales of his fur trade days. Like this one, as recounted by one of Oregon's writers, Robert Ormond Case:

"Sho! You call this bad weather? You call this trouble? You should have seen me and Milton Sublette one time, up in the Tetons. We were afoot, we had no victuals, and after I'd carried Sublette on my back for eight days —"

"Now wait," his listener said. "Why carry him on your back, Joe?"

18

Joseph L. Meek

"His leg was broke! And him a potbellied critter weighing two hundred and fifty pounds! D'ye know what shape my feet was in when we finally got to camp? Well, sir, I set ol' Sublette down and took a look. I'd been wondering why I'd been sinking to my ankles at each step, and now I see why. All I had left was ankles! For the last forty miles my feet had been worn off clean to the instep!"

Needless to say, the homesteader's evening was brightened considerably; he had gained a little strength for tomorrow's battles against a hard life on a stubborn earth.

For some time, the settlers in the Willamette Valley had felt the need of some sort of organized government. There were unfriendly Indians to contend with, for one thing. For another, wolves had plagued the homesteaders and an agency was needed to pay bounties to wolf hunters. In addition, Ewing Young, who owned much of the Chehalem Valley, had died and a government of some kind was needed to dispose legally of his huge estate.

By nightfall on May 1, 1843, a fairly large group had gathered at Champoeg, a settlement on the Willamette River about halfway between Oregon City and Salem. As was Joe Meek's habit, he circulated to talk up a report which a committee was to present the next day. The report called for the forming of a "provisional" government. It was hoped that this temporary government would lead toward Oregon's becoming part of the United States.

There were, in general, two types of early settlers in the Willamette Valley. In one group were the mountain men, like Joe Meek and Ewing Young, who had left the dying fur trade to take up a new life as farmers; in this group also were the missionaries, such as Jason Lee, who had come to the Oregon country to make Christians of heathen Indians; there were the farming men, too, who had been drawn to Oregon by the glowing promise of free and fertile land.

The second group was made up largely of retired employees of the Hudson's Bay Company; these were mostly French Canadians. The Hudson's Bay Company was a British fur trading concern represented in the Pacific Northwest by Dr. John McLoughlin at his post across the Columbia River at Vancouver.

In a sense, what was happening at Champoeg in May of 1843 could be boiled down to a contest between two men — Dr. McLoughlin and Joe Meek. McLoughlin was one man Meek had

Dr. John McLoughlin

never been able to charm with his outlandish talk. When Meek called at McLoughlin's Vancouver post, he was treated coolly.

McLoughlin admired serious, hard-working men; he was such a man himself.

Joe Meek was perhaps the least serious man in the Oregon country and he treated hard work as if it were a deadly disease.

And so the battle lines were drawn — Meek vs. McLoughlin, with all Oregon as the prize...

* * * * *

May 2, 1843, dawned at Champoeg with Joe Meek confident of victory. After a long night of palaver, as only Joe could palaver, he was convinced that these settlers were determined to form a government here and now... and he was just as convinced that the government would be American, not Canadian or British.

He was so thoroughly convinced, in fact that after the committee report had been delivered to the settlers assembled in a Hudson's Bay granary and solemn speeches had been made by others, Joe Meek spoke... and kept it short, for one of the few times in his tongue-wagging life. But for once, loafing got him into trouble.

Because somehow, somewhere, something went wrong...

Meek had expected wholehearted acclaim for the motion to form a provisional government leading toward becoming a territory of the United States.

Instead, there seemed to be more "Nays" than "Yeas."

"Thunderation!" bellowed Joe as the vote's echoes died. "Where did all them tea-drinkers come from?"

Then George LeBreton, a committee member, moved that the house be divided. In other words, he asked for a separation so that a head count could be made.

Some of those present had assumed that the meeting was over and left the building.

Joe Meek, dressed in his beaded vest and wearing his tattered buckskins and sputtering through his thick black beard, leaped up and roared in a voice that shook the Cascade Mountains, "Who's for a divide? All in favor of this here report and for organizing this here government, you jest follow me!"

The Americans and even a few French Canadians followed Joe Meek as he lined up on one side of the chairman.

Leaderless, the pro-Britain group lined up on the other side.

The count was made...

The minutes of the meeting don't record the actual count but reports indicate that there were fifty votes against organization of a provisional government which leaned toward America... and FIFTY-TWO for!

Joe Meek had won!

The United States had won!

Oregon had turned a corner; it had become American and was to remain American.

Naturally, Joe Meek led the victory cheer.

Public relations had scored its first victory on the West Coast.

* * * * *

Joseph L. Meek was appointed sheriff of most of the Oregon country. It didn't seem to disturb him in the least that the exact boundaries of his domain weren't established; there was still some doubt as to where Canada ended and the United States began.

But provisional government was only a start. The next step, a necessary one, was to convince the powers in Washington, D. C., that Oregon should be made a territory of the United States, with all of the rights and privileges pertaining thereto.

Provisional governor George Abernethy chose J. Quinn Thornton to travel by sea to present Oregon's case in Washington, D. C.

The legislature, on the other hand, chose Joe Meek. (No doubt Joe had made some impression on legislators by reminding them that he just happened to be a cousin of President James K. Polk.)

The legislature voted Meek $500 for expense money. There is some indication that Joe spent most of it in grateful celebration with his friends before he left Oregon. But Joe didn't worry, not for one minute.

After all, since when did Joe Meek need money to make his way cross-country, even in midwinter on horseback?

Didn't he have friends in the mountains? Of course he did.

Didn't he have the glorious title of "Envoy Extraordinary and Minister Plenipotentiary from the Republic of Oregon to the

Court of the United States?'' Of course he did.

Didn't he have the Joe Meek mouth? Of course he did.

* * * * *

All of these came in handy before he reached Washington. After a wild trip enlivened with near-starvation, Indian trouble and utter poverty, he reached St. Louis, which was then still the western outpost of American civilization.

He needed steamboat passage from St. Louis but he had no money to pay for it. Two competing steamboats were at the docks. Joe leaped onto the hurricane deck of one of them, which seemed to his practiced free-loading eye to offer the best accomodations, and bellowed to a throng of prospective passengers on shore, ''Over here, folks! Board the 'Declaration!' Finest food and drink and beds for all! You've read about me in the papers — the man from the Oregon country, Envoy Extraordinary and Minister Plenipotentiary to the President of the United States, my cousin James K. Polk!''

The ''Declaration'' got most of the customers. Joe Meek got free passage and the best of treatment from a grateful skipper for as long as he remained aboard the stately vessel.

But he finally had to leave this lovely craft and board a train. The conductor asked him for a ticket. Joe answered in the Snake Indian tongue and, to the delight of the passengers, rode free.

He reached Washington in due course. It just happened that President Polk's private secretary, a young man named Knox Walker, also was a relative of Meek's. Joe had little trouble in arranging to see the president.

In short order, President Polk sent a message to Congress urging that Oregon be admitted as a territory of the United States.

J. Quinn Thornton was there, too, and was seated officially in the solemn halls of Congress as a delegate from Oregon.

Joe Meek did his work in the cloakrooms, talking...

History does not agree upon which man from Oregon accomplished more, Thornton, the quiet-spoken, suave official delegate, or Joseph L. Meek, the bearded frontier envoy extraordinary... VERY extraordinary.

But history does record that Oregon officially became a territory of the United States government on August 14, 1848, during the last few hours of the Congressional session.

The Chinese say that one picture is worth ten thousand words. Well ... perhaps.

But not if they were Joe Meek words.

THE BACKGROUND

As Joe Meek might have expressed it, Dr. John McLoughlin, a giant figure in Oregon history, was a man "caught between a rock and a hard place."

Between 1825, when McLoughlin established Fort Vancouver as an outpost of the British-owned Hudson's Bay Company, and 1843, when the provisional government was established at Champoeg, the Canadian fur king pretty much ruled the roost in the Oregon country.

The "rock" was Dr. McLoughlin's responsibility to his employer; the "hard place" was his sympathy for the American settlers as they straggled into the Willamette Valley. When McLoughlin helped the settlers, he angered his employer. If he did not help them, he wounded his own conscience and earned the settlers' hate.

Eventually, this conflict resulted in his resignation from Hudson's Bay Company in 1845. He became an American citizen and built a fine house in Oregon City, which remains to this day as a National Historical Site.

He made his choice, difficult though it was. Even so, he must have felt at his death in 1857 that he had been crushed between the rock and the hard place.

The British no longer trusted him because he had helped the Americans; Americans were suspicious of him because he had been a British citizen. In 1849, he was stripped of all of his land holdings in Oregon by federal action. The man who had opened up the Oregon country was to go to his grave under the Church of St. John in Oregon City as the owner of none of it.

Then, five years after Dr. McLoughlin's death, the conscience of Oregon returned ownership of the land to his heirs by special legislation. It is one of the great sadnesses of Oregon history that the "Father of Oregon" did not live to appreciate the thankful act. (The "Father of Oregon" title, incidentally, was made official in 1957, when the state legislature chose to recognize Dr. McLoughlin's work by giving him this honorary name.)

McLoughlin house

No such sadness surrounded the last years of Joe Meek. After cutting his wide swath through Washington, D. C., he returned to Oregon all puffed up with the title of United States Marshal. He had a wonderful time for a while wandering over the Oregon Territory carrying out his official duties. (And, Joe being Joe, undoubtedly a few unofficial ones, too.) He even discarded his buckskins out of respect for his new position and acquired regular trousers and a coat with brass buttons.

He died in 1875. The funeral at his homestead north of Hillsboro was attended by nearly 500 persons. For its day, this was remarkable. But then, Joe was a most remarkable man. He was buried near the lovely Old Scotch Church (Tualatin Plains Presbyterian) a few miles north of Hillsboro, where his headstone may be seen today.

The original Oregon Territory proclaimed in 1848 stretched from the Rocky Mountains to the Pacific Ocean between the 42nd

Newell house

and 49th parallels. General Joseph Lane of Indiana was appointed its first governor. In 1853, the area was made much smaller by the splitting off of Washington Territory. What was left of Oregon Territory is what we call the state of Oregon today.

Statehood was achieved on February 14, 1859, when President Buchanan signed the bill in Washington, D. C., but the news didn't reach Portland until March 15. The organization of the state government was completed on May 16, 1859. In 1864, Oregon voters chose Salem as the state capital.

Champoeg Memorial State Park marks the site of the 1843 meeting which resulted in an American provisional government. A museum here contains many relics of the old days. Near the gates of the park is the home of Robert Newell, who came out of the mountains with Joe Meek. Built in 1852, the house was the only one in the town of Champoeg which survived a Willamette River flood in 1861. It is now owned and maintained by the Daughters of the American Revolution.

Many other buildings remain to remind modern Oregonians of the old days. At St. Paul stands the first church in Oregon to be built of brick. The cornerstone was laid in 1846. Enlarged and remodelled, it is still in use.

Oregon's steamboating tycoon, Captain John C. Ainsworth, has left his landmark, too, with a stately white house in the Mt. Pleasant section of Oregon City. The house looks much as it did in the days when the King of the River called it home.

Most of Oregon's historic buildings are in the northern part of the Willamette Valley; there, after all, is where early settlement was heaviest. The Oregon City-Milwaukie area is particularly rich ground; the Tualatin and Chehalem Valleys, in and around the triangle formed by Hillsboro, Forest Grove and Newberg, are also productive for a miner of history.

Of special interest is the Minthorn House in Newberg, built in 1881 by Jesse Edwards. Herbert Hoover, elected President of the United States in 1928, lived in this house as a boy. No other Oregon home has been so honored. The house was bought by Dr. Henry John Minthorn, Hoover's uncle, in 1884, shortly after the young orphan named Herbert Hoover came west to live with the Minthorns.

In 1955, the Minthorn House was opened to the public. Former President Hoover, then 81, came from New York for the occasion.

Ainsworth house

In southern Oregon, travellers along Interstate 5 need merely glance to the west side of the highway at Wolf Creek in Josephine County to see a stage station once operated by Ben Holladay.

The unpainted, vine-covered Birdseye home, built in 1856, still stands south of the Rogue River Highway in Jackson County. In 1965, Mrs. Effie Birdseye, daughter-in-law of the builder, was still enjoying the warmth of the fireplace which heated the home more than 100 years ago.

So some of the old homes, which once echoed to the trials and triumphs of pioneer life, still stand and there suddenly is hope that they will remain through another hundred years. In 1933, the federal government surveyed, photographed and measured 42 of these old buildings. In 1964, less than half still stood, but the Oregon Landmarks Committee was organized by the Oregon Historical Society. Legislation was passed to permit the state to take over and maintain the old homes for the benefit of those modern Oregonians who don't want to forget the past because they recognize and value its place in the present.

SUGGESTED READING

Bronson, Lynn; THE RUNAWAY; Lippincott; 1953.

Garst, Shannon; JOE MEEK, MAN OF THE WEST; Messner; 1954.

Johnson, Jalmar; BUILDERS OF THE NORTHWEST; Dodd, Mead; 1963.

Lampman, Evelyn Sibley; PRINCESS OF FORT VANCOUVER; Doubleday; 1962.

Lundy, Jo Evalin; THE CHALLENGERS; Aladdin; 1953.

OREGON HISTORIC LANDMARKS; Oregon Society, Daughters of the American Revolution; 1963.

Tobie, Harvey Elmer; NO MAN LIKE JOE; Binfords & Mort-Oregon Historical Society; 1949.

CHAPTER THREE – The Oregon Trail:
A NOBLE FOOL

The small train of wagons left The Dalles early on that September morning of 1845 and rolled easily south over autumn brown hills toward Tygh Valley.

On their right, looming in crisp majesty against a morning-blue sky, was the snow-capped enemy — Mt. Hood. Still, while some members of the party feared this mountain as they had feared nothing else in their long journey across the wide land, they talked of Mt. Hood's awesome beauty and felt a glow of pleasure around the edges of their fear. If all went well, they reminded themselves, they would live out their lives within sight of this proud sentinel in the sky.

Ahead of the wagon train, squinting against the yellow harshness of the early light, rode a tall, lean, sharp-faced Kentuckian who was about to experience the most noble moments of his 55 years.

The man was Samuel Kimbrough Barlow. He left The Dalles with cries of "fool" ringing in his ears, but he was soon to arrive in the annals of Oregon history with a different name, that of "pathfinder."

Mountain men, wise in the windings of the Indian trails through the Cascade Mountains, had joined in calling him fool. It was impossible, they said, to take a wagon train with women and children through the mountains into the Willamette Valley.

"The Lord," said Sam Barlow with his thin lips turning down at the edges, "never made a mountain but what he made a way to get around it."

Strong words. Stubborn words. And even, perhaps, foolish words.

"The Lord," retorted the mountain men at The Dalles, "never said ary word about wagons."

But Sam Barlow was a man who was born to ignore advice. (It is surprising how many historic figures shared this trait.) It seemed to him, when he had studied the area around Mt. Hood as the train came out of the Blue Mountains to the east weeks earlier, that there was a gap to the south of the looming mountain called Hood. It is quite likely that in that moment, even before the wagons of the Barlow train had reached The Dalles on the

Samuel K. Barlow

south bank of the Columbia River, Captain Barlow decided on the plan which was to earn him his place in the history of the Oregon Trail.

If modern highway practice had been followed, there would have been a sign along the Oregon Trail at The Dalles which said: "Dead End." There was no pass through the Cascade Mountains which would allow passage for wagons. The only route to the Promised Land of the Willamette Valley, the only means by which emigrants could finally reach the free black dirt which offered a good life for generations to come, was the mighty Columbia River, which ran through a great slot now known as Columbia Gorge on its last angry lunge toward the sea.

Profiteers, feeding on the land-hunger of the emigrants, charged high prices for passage. At this late point on the Oregon Trail, emigrant funds were usually low, having been drained away by the hundreds of hard miles they had travelled to this place called The Dalles.

But some paid, then suffered terribly as the raging rapids of the Columbia often up-ended the boats, scattered prize possessions and ended the lives of men, women and children. Some paid only after selling the goods they had hauled painfully over almost 2000 miles. Some built rafts of logs to save passage money, then, ignorant of the river's cruel ways, embarked in the surging currents, sometimes perishing amid the jagged rocks.

The deadly threat of the river route discouraged even as stubborn a man as Sam Barlow. It seemed to him that there had to be a better way to reach the green land which awaited them. They had come overland through a brutal summer; now to throw these hard-won hundreds of miles into the maw of the river seemed like suicide.

"I'll start overland tomorrow with my family and my wagons," said Sam Barlow at The Dalles. "All those who don't know the meaning of 'can't' are welcome to join. We'll leave the rest behind."

* * * * *

On the bright day which followed, there were about a dozen wagons rolling away from The Dalles. The core of the train was the Barlow family: Susannah Lee, Sam's wife; William, 22, his oldest son; James and John, his younger sons, and Mrs. Albert (Sarah) Gaines, a married daughter. All told, there were 19

33

adults, an indefinite number of children, 16 yoke of cattle, seven horses and one dog.

The train rolled southward from The Dalles through open country for a time, then stopped for rest and repair of wagons. Sam Barlow chose not to rest. Instead he moved ahead to scout the route through the foothills of the Cascades.

While Barlow was gone, an important party of late-starters caught up. This party's leader was Joel Palmer, a frontier-wise Canadian who was to earn an important place in Oregon history. He brought approximately 23 wagons with him, thus more than doubling the size of the group. Palmer knew Sam Barlow; Palmer's party had accompanied Barlow's for at least part of the long trail which led to The Dalles.

Barlow soon returned from his scouting mission with an encouraging report: No great obstacles lay in their path. It was true that the Indian trail which they would follow had not been travelled by wagons. In certain places where large trees had fallen across the route, Indians had merely chopped out a notch through which their ponies could jump. All that was needed, Barlow said, was more axe work.

Apparently some members of the party decided that their axes were too dull and rusty, their men too weak. They headed back to The Dalles to take their chances on the river. Others, though, including Joel Palmer, decided to play along with Sam Barlow. Some of the party went back to get supplies for the assault on the mountain trail. Barlow, Palmer and a man named Lock stepped out toward the mountain for more poking around in the trouble which lay ahead.

The wagon train bestirred itself and pushed on. The sun still shone warmly; the way still was easy. Then appeared William Rector and his party, hurrying from The Dalles to catch up. His wife was "sickly," as they said in those days, but she had a bright and active mind, and was an asset to the pioneering party.

Meanwhile, on the shoulder of the mountain . . .

* * * * *

Barlow, Palmer and Lock had labored toward the Cascade trail summit. When they stood upon it, a vast expanse of timber, as thick as hair upon a dog, reached away toward the Promised Land.

34

Original Barlow Road

Searching for an easier way around the steep ravine they had crossed earlier, Palmer climbed high on the snowy mountain, while Barlow and Lock recrossed at a lower elevation. Then the three men rejoined and made their way back to the main party late at night.

In the morning, the party held a conclave around a warming fire. After further exploration, an agreement was reached. While wagons could pass, it would be a difficult road. With winter threatening, the wise course seemed to be to push as far as they could with wagons, then move down into the valley afoot and on horseback; the wagons with their loads of prized possessions could be brought out in the spring and summer.

Barlow, Palmer and Lock had found near the summit of the pass an open place which they called Summit Prairie. It was decided that the wagon train would proceed toward this point. If it then seemed wise, a cabin would be erected for the storage of goods and shelter for the guarding party.

Palmer, the William Buffums and Mrs. Arthur Thompson set out on horseback for Oregon City, planning to secure provisions and more riding horses for the party.

Barlow and Rector set off on foot for the same purpose. Apparently during this journey, with provisions running low and fatigue running high, William Rector formed a low opinion of Sam Barlow. Barlow was 55 years old; Rector was 40. Between that span of 15 years is a great gulf of energy and endurance. Sam Barlow had made two scouting trips already; this was Rector's first trip. In later years, Rector claimed Barlow was more hindrance than help on this trip.

They set out into the forested wilderness. They crossed the summit and started down into the valley. Obstacles arose on every side; the timber was thick and threatening; the canyons were steep and clogged with rock; the snow-fed streams were swift and dangerous.

They stumbled onto canyons which seemed impassable for wagons. Searching for a pass, they wandered up and down the ridges, gullies and canyons for nearly a week and finally, with their supplies running low, decided to plunge straight ahead into the valley to get food for themselves and for the wagon train which was straining to follow the blazed trail.

Behind them, the wagons slogged upward. Swamps were encountered which bogged wagons down; at times men worked for hours in the mud to gain only a few precious yards. As one difficult day followed another without word from those who had gone ahead, spirits began to sink. Lack of leadership began to be felt. While the record is not clear on this point, it is likely that the size of the party shrank steadily as wagons were turned around by their disheartened owners and headed back for The Dalles.

Then, one fine day, a shout rang through the trees.

Sam Barlow and William Rector had returned!

They brought supplies from Oregon City and more important, they brought leadership. Morale improved quickly; plans were made and work renewed. All lingering hopes that wagons might soon be brought down the mountainside were forgotten; the west slope was forested much more heavily than the east; the canyons were deeper and wider; the streams ran white with rushing water.

William Rector, worried about his sick wife, decided to return to The Dalles with his family; the trip down the west slope, with winter sweeping into the high places, would be too difficult for Mrs. Rector. It is likely that a few other families joined the Rectors, although again the record is unclear.

Preparations went ahead at a hurried pace. The threat of snow blockade grew with each passing day of late November. It was decided William Barlow and William Berry would remain at the cabin, called "Fort Deposit," for the winter to guard the wagons. Then, when it became plain that food enough for only one person could be spared, Berry volunteered to stay alone. (One account of this period reports that all of the reading matter of the group was contributed to Berry as a means to stave off cabin fever during the long winter which lay ahead.)

Sam Barlow supervised the loading of the expedition's horses, then led the way as the three families still at Fort Deposit — the Barlows, the Caplingers and the Gaineses — moved off into the dark forest on the last hard leg of their trip to the Promised Land.

The terrors of the west slope lay ahead, including the infamous Laurel Hill, which proved to be painfully difficult even without wagons.

A foot of snow brought into the open the panic which some members of the party felt. With winter well upon them and their

37

supplies again running low, Mrs. Caplinger and others began to speak their fears.

"We'll freeze," moaned Mrs. Caplinger. "If we don't freeze, we'll starve!"

"Nonsense," replied Mrs. Gaines, Barlow's oldest child. "Why, we're in the midst of plenty! Plenty of snow, plenty of wood to melt it, plenty of horse meat, plenty of dog meat if the worst comes."

As a safety measure, William Barlow and another young man, John Bacon, were sent ahead to get supplies at Oregon City. They were then to return to meet the descending main party.

William Barlow sped ahead of Bacon on the route to the settlement, got supplies and spent the night at the Foster home. Early the next morning, William started out to rescue the pioneering party.

To his great surprise and delight, he met them before evening, wearily slogging through the foothills.

After resting for a time at the Foster home, the Barlow party pushed on to Oregon City, arriving on Christmas Day, 1845.

The wagons belonging to the party were not brought over the trail until July and August of the next year.

The last link in the Oregon Trail had been forged. A monument to human courage had been carved through the Cascade wilderness.

If Sam Barlow was a fool, he was a noble fool.

THE BACKGROUND

The Oregon Trail ... the words have come down in American history swathed in glory, steeped in legend.

The legends make good reading but the facts are fascinating enough. American Indians, astounded at the sight of seemingly endless trains of whitetopped wagons passing in lines which stretched to either horizon, supposedly called the trail "The Great Medicine Road of the Whites."

In its early stages, at least, the great migration might well have been called "The Trek of the Children." The first large train moved west from Independence, Missouri, in 1843, with almost 900 people. Approximately 600 of those were youngsters.

Original Oregon Trail south of Vale

The youngest were tucked into the wagons; those who were older walked alongside; some rode horses. They gathered firewood; they tended livestock; they picked flowers and played games. (South of Arlington, in Gilliam County, is a marker at a trail crossing which honors W. W. Weatherford, who, as a boy of 17, drove oxen west in 1861. Nothing unusual about that, except that young Weatherford did it barefoot.)

What lured these people west? The prospect of free land certainly was one attraction. But there was free or almost-free land also to be had in 1843 in the country from which they started, the area we now call the Midwest.

Gold? This precious metal was not to be discovered in quantity until later.

Were they in such terrible condition in their old homes that any change would be an improvement? Not so. Most were farmers, businessmen and craftsmen, successful by the standards of their day, with money and possessions.

They must have been reckless adventurers then, persons born to take a chance for the thrill of chance-taking. Not likely. There were few footloose bachelors in the early migrations; most of the adult males were solid family men. One needs only to count again the children in the party of 1843 to prove this.

They came, most of them, simply because they wanted to, because they were driven by the pioneering instinct which crops out again and again beside the long trail of American history. They were driven by optimism; life was good, but it could be better. They were driven by curiosity; life was interesting but what fascinating sights, do you suppose, lie beyond yonder hill? (Americans remain, to this day, the most travelling people on earth.)

They were heading into a wilderness where few white men had gone before. But it must be remembered that the country from which they came was considered raw frontier at the time. They would not have been where they were if they had been afraid of making their own way in a new land.

The Great Migration headed west in May of 1843 across the prairies of what is now Nebraska. The timing was sensible; in fact it was essential if the wagons were to cross the western mountains before the next winter's snows. They followed the Platte River for a time, then had to cross it. The crossing was a hard, week-long job.

Fort Laramie, in what is now Wyoming, was reached by the middle of July. They had to cross the Platte again before continuing westward up the Sweetwater River to Independence Rock, which remains as the most famous landmark of the trip.

By this time, most of them had recovered from the fear of Indian attack which had haunted their dreams on the early legs of the journey. There seemed to be more friendly warriors than savage ones. In fact, over the long history of travel over the Oregon Trail, there is no positive record of a single mass Indian attack on a wagon train, movies and television to the contrary.

A much greater hazard was a disease called cholera; it left its victims along the trail by the hundreds. (This harsh aspect of trail life shaped the personalities of many who were later to become famous in Oregon. The mother of Abigail Scott Duniway, for instance, died along the Oregon Trail. There is no doubt that the cruel fate of her mother, who had started the journey in a frail, work-worn condition, later spurred Mrs. Duniway to her tremendous effort in the cause of women's rights. Her brother Harvey Scott, who had also travelled the trail with his family to become Oregon's most respected newspaper editor, was likewise unable to shake from his mind the trail-side death of his mother.)

On July 30, the travellers saw the feared Rocky Mountains and marvelled at the mid-summer cap of snow. They crossed South Pass and found it not so difficult after all. Suddenly all streams ran west; they had crossed the Continental Divide. They stopped at Fort Bridger, then at a Hudson's Bay trading post bearing the name of Ft. Hall. (Many later trains were to turn southwest here for California.)

The men at Ft. Hall did not encourage the emigrants; they doubted that wagons could be brought through to the Columbia River. Luckily, a leader of the train was Dr. Marcus Whitman, the missionary of Wailatpu. He had been over the trail, but not with wagons. However, he was sure that wagons could pass.

The train moved on, apparently undiscouraged. The hardships of the trail, however, had splintered the group; now the train broke into groups of families and close friends. They crossed Snake River, Burnt River and Powder River and finally were in the Grande Ronde Valley of Oregon.

The Blue Mountains lay ahead. The assault was started. As the winter's first snow fell, the wagons rolled over the crest and

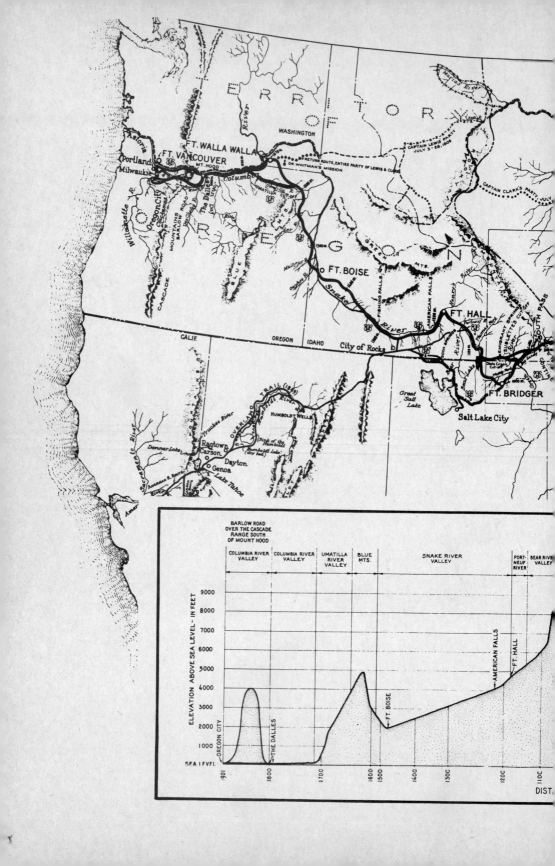

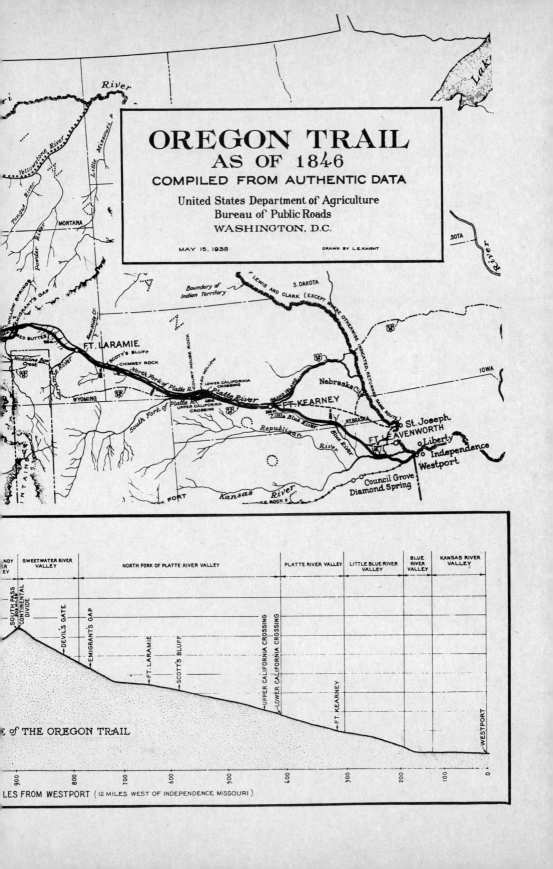

OREGON TRAIL
AS OF 1846
COMPILED FROM AUTHENTIC DATA

United States Department of Agriculture
Bureau of Public Roads
WASHINGTON, D.C.

MAY 15, 1938   DRAWN BY L.E.KNIGHT

down into the Umatilla Valley. Some wagons turned toward the Columbia, where rafts were built for the journey down the mighty river. Others pushed on to the Dalles, only delaying the moment when the Columbia had to be faced. (This, remember, was in 1843; Sam Barlow didn't come along until two years later.)

Most of the members of that first large train licked their wounds at Ft. Vancouver, the Hudson's Bay headquarters of Dr. John McLoughlin, then crossed the river into the Willamette Valley.

They had come 1800 miles from Independence; the trip required more than five months. (Much the same route can be driven today in three days, with the major difficulty being the finding of good music on the radio.)

There had been earlier travellers who followed Lewis and Clark over the trail to Oregon: the missionaries, Whitman, Henry Spaulding, Jason Lee, Elijah White and Father Pierre De Smet; the mountain men, Joel Walker, Joe Meek and Robert Newell; the explorers, Captain John C. Fremont, Captain Benjamin Bonneville and Nathaniel Wyeth.

Those whose arrival in 1843 doubled the population found that some of the earlier arrivals had already formed a loose government; the foundation was there; the work of expansion could begin.

Word of the success of the 1843 migration travelled east as rapidly as the communication of the time allowed.

More came during the next year; in 1845, 3000 came, including the Barlow family. Travel over the now-rutted path continued in rising and falling waves until 1869, when the first transcontinental railroad was finished.

One of the leaders of the 1843 expedition, Jesse Applegate, pushed south soon after to found the Applegate Trail, which, when it became known, was to carry as many wagons as the northern route in the great human flood which flowed toward the west.

But what of Sam Barlow? Soon after arriving at Oregon City, he petitioned the Oregon territorial legislature for a charter to open a toll road over the path he had scouted. The charter was granted; after taking in a partner, Phillip Foster, Barlow and a crew began the work of clearing a wagon trail in the spring of 1846. In October of that year, 152 wagons and 1500 head of livestock came over the new road.

44

Columbia River and Mt. Hood from east of The Dalles

Some say that Barlow enriched himself from tolls on the historic road; it is not likely. The tourist season along the Barlow Road was very short. The record shows that he gave up the road after two years, when he felt that he had gotten back the cost of clearing it. The road passed through a succession of operators in the years to come but remained as the last important link of the Oregon Trail.

The last few years of Barlow's life were spent at Canemah, a river landing south of Oregon City, where he died in 1867. He was buried in a cemetery at the village of Barlow in Clackamas County. His grave marker can be found there today.

Samuel Kimbrough Barlow has not been forgotten. A bronze tablet in his memory was placed near Government Camp by the Sons and Daughters of the Pioneers. The route of the Mt. Hood Loop highway as it climbs east around the shoulder of the mighty mountain follows in some places the old route of the historic wagon trail.

Barlow, Applegate, Whitman . . . the names echo through Oregon history. They came west because they wanted to. Many of us followed along the modern Oregon Trail for no better reason and have no more cause for regret than they.

We know why they came; we know why they stayed to build.

SUGGESTED READING

Allen, Eleanor; CANVAS CARAVANS; Binfords & Mort; 1946.

American Heritage; WESTWARD ON THE OREGON TRAIL; American Heritage; 1962.

Beard, Chaplain John W.; SADDLES EAST; Binfords & Mort; 1949.

Judson, Katherine Berry; EARLY DAYS IN OLD OREGON; Binfords & Mort; 1954.

Lampman, Evelyn Sibley; TREE WAGON; Doubleday; 1953.

Powers, Alfred; TRUE ADVENTURES ON WESTWARD TRAILS; Little Brown; 1954.

Salisbury, Albert and Jane; HERE ROLLED THE COVERED WAGONS; Superior; 1948.

Webb, Todd; THE GOLD RUSH TRAIL AND THE ROAD TO OREGON; Doubleday; 1963.

CHAPTER FOUR – The Indians:
JOSEPH, STATESMAN-WARRIOR

The tall Indian rose and let his worn blanket fall from his shoulders. A respectful silence settled over the other Nez Perce leaders assembled in solemn council.

Before speaking, Joseph turned for a long look toward his beloved Wallowa country of eastern Oregon, the Land of Winding Waters, already many hard miles behind them.

He feared that if Looking Glass and White Bird and other chiefs had their way, the homeland of Joseph's small band would fade forever into the great distances of memory. Then the bones of Joseph's father, which he had sworn to protect, would be left unguarded in the grave near Wallowa Lake.

Once, only weeks before, Joseph had sadly concluded that flight from their ancestral homeland was a wise decision. But he had not foreseen the recent battle-scarred days; he had not expected that the Nez Perce would be forced to travel so far from their familiar haunts.

Now even Toohoolhoolzote, veteran of many battles, seemed to be weary of fighting. He and other influential leaders, Joseph knew, wanted only to flee to Canada to escape the gathering swarms of soldiers. In Canada, argued those who wanted to run, the Nez Perce might make a new life by joining the exiled band of the mighty Plains Indians, the Sioux led by Sitting Bull.

The Nez Perce had scored a startling victory over the bluecoats in White Bird Canyon, but the sweet taste of it had plainly faded.

Joseph understood the feeling of those who wanted to flee, even if he did not share it. He had left his ancient homeland with great reluctance; he felt that leaving would avoid much bloodshed. But now it was plain that the whites intended to drive the Nez Perce far from their lands...or wipe them out.

The deathbed entreaty of his father, Old Joseph, was carved into his conscience:

"When I am gone, think of your country. You are chief of these peoples. They look to you to guide them. Always remember that your father never sold his country. You must stop your ears whenever you are asked to sign a treaty selling your home. A few years more, and the white men will be all around you. They have their eyes on this land. My son, never forget my dying words. This country holds your father's body. Never sell the bones of your father and mother."

Haunted by these words, Young Joseph faced the other Nez Perce leaders with determination.

"What are we fighting for?" asked Joseph, his eyes seeking out those who were truly listening. "Is it for our lives? No! It is for this land where the bones of our fathers are buried. I do not want to take my women among strangers. I do not want to die in a strange land. Some of you tried to say, once, that I was afraid of the whites. You wanted fighting. Stay here with me now and you shall have plenty of fighting. We will put our women behind us in these mountains, and die on our own land fighting for them. I would rather do that than run I know not where."

Then Joseph sat down.

The council voted; the vote went against Joseph.

With a heavy heart, Joseph started with the others up the Lolo Trail toward Canada. Thus began one of the most difficult and courageous treks in the history of freedom-loving humanity.

*****

As they climbed through the mountains along the Lolo Trail, the Nez Perce carried a proud history with them. French-Canadian trappers of the David Thompson's Canadian North West Company had given them the name "Nez Perce," French for "pierced nose," because some of them liked to wear ornaments in their noses. The Indians did not care for the name. Nevertheless, the tribe became known by it. The old name, "Shahaptian," fell into disuse.

48

Old Joseph's grave at Wallowa Lake

It was a proud boast of the Nez Perce that they had never killed a white man. They had often shown eagerness to take on white ways. Generally whites had discovered the Nez Perce to be intelligent and friendly. When Lewis and Clark's band of explorers, hungry and weary, descended upon their land, the Nez Perce had given what help they could. Apparently many Nez Perce made a serious effort to adopt Christianity, even sending representatives as far as St. Louis in search of Christian teachers who would come to live with them. It is believed that Old Joseph was married by Rev. Spaulding at the Whitman Mission and that Young Joseph was baptized by him a year later.

Then the pattern of peace was rudely shattered. Cayuse Indians, with real and fancied grievances against the Whitmans, massacred them. Many missions were closed as fear spread through the white communities.

Settlers all over the Pacific Northwest cried out for help. Swarms of United States Cavalry answered the call.

Hoping to stay clear of the trouble, Young Joseph and his little band of Nez Perce retreated into the mountains around Wallowa Lake. Still the pressure mounted as white settlers continued to stream over the Oregon Trail.

Even so, Joseph's band, locked in its mountain home, managed to escape warfare.

Then gold was discovered on their land!

Treasure-hungry trespassers stormed into the Nez Perce country, plundering and murdering in their lust for gold. Towns sprang up, forcing Joseph's people even farther into the mountains.

Now government representatives appeared with offers to move the Indians to new land. It seemed to Joseph that always less land was offered in exchange, and poorer land as well. The whites, always squeezing and pinching, seemed determined to shrink the hallowed Mother Earth of the Nez Perce religion; trespassing and stealing by whites continued.

Joseph, as always, displayed the patience of a great man. Peace was a part of his life; only through peace, he knew, could he live out that life in the lovely land where his father was buried; only through peace could his people survive in the lush valleys and soaring mountains which had seen their birth and nurtured their good life.

The Nez Perce had a strong case; some wise men in the white man's government supported them and issued orders prohibiting further white settlement. But the gold lust was too strong; settlers ignored the orders and flocked to the Wallowa Valley.

Young Joseph appealed to Indian agents for relief. An order was issued by President U. S. Grant to the white settlers in the valley: Withdraw. The land henceforth was to be considered a "reservation for the roaming Nez Perce Indians."

It sounded like what Joseph wanted for his people but the sound became hollow when the U. S. Congress reversed Grant's decision. A parley was called by General Oliver O. Howard and agents from Washington. The goal was a "permanent" agreement between the white government and the Indians.

Joseph was prominent and outspoken at the parley. The whites found that they could sway some Nez Perce leaders, among them the chief they called "Lawyer." But Joseph was magnificently immovable. His arguments were intelligent and vigorous. Perhaps for the first time, the whites appreciated the meaning of Joseph's Indian name: "Thunder Rolling in the Mountains."

An agreement was reached with Lawyer, who said that he represented all of the Nez Perce. The feature of the agreement which angered Joseph was a simple one: The Wallowa Lake country was not included in the reservation. It was easy for Lawyer to accept such an agreement; his band did not live in the Wallowa country; his own homeland was included in the proposed reservation. It surely was not difficult for Lawyer to give away land he did not own.

The white negotiators, naturally, were delighted with Lawyer's attitude and with his signature on the treaty of 1863. Joseph was not.

Joseph infuriated the whites by saying, "If we ever owned the land we own it still, for we never sold it. In the treaty councils the commissioners have claimed that our country has been sold to the government. Suppose a white man should come to me and say, 'Joseph, I like your horses, and I want to buy them.' I say to him, 'No, my horses suit me, I will not sell them.' Then he goes to my neighbor, and says to him, 'Joseph has some good horses. I want to buy them but he refuses to sell.' My neighbor answers, 'Pay me the money, and I will sell you Joseph's horses.' The white man returns to me and says, 'Joseph, I have bought

51

your horses and you must let me have them.' If we sold our lands to the government, this is the way they were bought."

Further agreements were made. Again they were broken, usually by the whites. Joseph's warriors were becoming increasingly restless and angry. Constantly Joseph had to argue for further patience. The sad moment finally arrived when Joseph realized that compromise was necessary if his small band were to survive. White power was too great; Joseph knew that the Nez Perce could not prevail against it.

He agreed to take his band across the Snake River to the Lapwai Agency in what is now western Idaho. Near Lapwai, three of Joseph's warriors finally exploded, rode out of camp and killed several whites. The warriors came back to camp full of boasts; they were joined by others. In the resulting rampage, more whites were killed.

The uneasy peace had been shattered forever. Joseph knew that his people must flee or be exterminated. They headed southeast toward White Bird Canyon and the first real battle the Nez Perce had ever fought against the white man.

* * * * *

Captain David Perry, leading his First Cavalry troop into White Bird Canyon, had every reason to believe that his star would rise at this early morning hour. He had about 90 soldiers under his command, plus a dozen or so civilian volunteers and a few Indians who had accepted treaties with the whites. He knew that the Nez Perce under Joseph probably had about the same number of warriors but they were poorly armed and surely no match for the bluecoats.

His confidence grew by the moment as he neared the Indian encampment at the bottom of the narrow canyon where White Bird Creek poured into the Salmon River. He saw smoke rising from Nez Perce campfires as advancing dawn smudged the canyon walls with streaks of yellow. His scouts had reported hurried movement in the camp but indications were that the Indians were preparing to flee, not fight.

He ordered his mounted soldiers into the canyon, with Lieutenant Edward Theller and a small advance party trotting one hundred yards ahead of the main body.

Captain Perry ordered his troops to block the canyon. His line broke into disorganized bits when Nez Perce warriors appeared like vengeful spirits from behind the rocks and smashed at the flanks, then thundered into the center.

The canyon quickly filled with smoke and dust. Captain Perry bellowed orders as his line faltered, then broke. Lieutenant Theller and 18 men were pocketed against the canyon wall and wiped out. The civilians ran like startled sheep and soldiers followed, streaming up the canyon.

Racing up the canyon after his command, Captain Perry tried to rally them on the plateau but the pursuing Nez Perce made a rally impossible.

The battle had lasted only a few minutes. Instead of surprising the Nez Perce, Captain Perry had fallen into a trap. A third of Perry's force was left for dead in White Bird Canyon. The Indians suffered only small losses and recovered from the battlefield a large number of badly-needed firearms.

As the news spread of the cavalry's shocking defeat in White Bird Canyon, alarm surged like fire in dry grass through the white settlements of the Northwest. With fear came puzzlement, which centered around the character of Joseph.

What could possibly have turned this peace-loving, statesmanlike Indian into the avenger of White Bird Canyon?

Only those who knew the full story of Joseph and the Nez Perce, of their long fight against white oppression, could come up with an answer.

* * * * *

In some ways, it was the strangest of wars.

By all reasonable standards, the Nez Perce should have quickly lost it. Much of the mighty force of Indian-fighting U. S. Cavalry was arrayed against them. General Howard with a substantial force trailed them; numerous army units summoned by telegraph tried to head them off; others bit at their flanks. The Nez Perce took with them all their women and children, their old and their sick, plus their belongings. The cavalry carried only the weapons of war.

The small band of Nez Perce which had scored such a resounding victory at White Bird was quickly strengthened as other Nez Perce war chiefs heard of the triumph and moved speedily to join the struggle. But even with the added strength, along the long road to Canada, Joseph usually fought against great odds . . . and

53

Joseph in 1877

often won.

After nine brutal days in the mountains along the Lolo Trail, Joseph and his people appeared in what is now western Montana, only to find a hastily-built stockade and a force of soldiers and civilians from Ft. Missoula blocking their passage.

Joseph, Looking Glass and White Bird came down from a ridge to parley under a flag of truce.

"We go toward the Crow Nation," Joseph said. "We wish to move in peace through the valley of the Bitterroot. We shall harm no one. We shall pay for food."

Swayed by Joseph's open manner, remembering his reputation for honesty, the volunteers voted to accept Joseph's terms. They decided to let him pass. Families of many of the volunteers lay in Joseph's path; they did not care to make the Nez Perce leader angry.

And so the Nez Perce slipped by the stockade, which was to come down through history with the name "Fort Fizzle."

Yes, it was a strange war. But the Nez Perce were a strange and noble people and their leader, Joseph, was a strange and noble man.

* * * * *

There were other battles, other skirmishes, as Joseph and his people pushed toward Canada, which, with each painful mile, looked more and more like a safe haven from their white tormentors. But now precious military reputations were at stake. Officers and soldiers whose sworn duty was protection of white settlers had been made to look foolish. Whites along the route of Joseph's march had begun to help him, to root for him, to laugh at the soldiers who floundered in the mountains all around the line of the Indian pilgrimage.

The United States Army finally found itself in the position of having to halt Joseph's flight... or destroy its own influence on the western frontier.

The turning point may have come at a campground along the Big Hole River, near what is now the Idaho-Montana border. Joseph ordered a halt; the Nez Perce rested. General Howard was still far back in the Bitterroots; trouble seemed far away.

Then the unsuspecting Nez Perce camp was attacked by a force under Colonel John Gibbon, who had rushed across country from Fort Shaw, on the Sun River.

The aging chief White Bird this time rallied the surprised Nez Perce as he cried, "Why are we retreating? Since the world was made, brave men have fought for their women and children! Fight! Shoot them down! We can shoot as well as any of these soldiers!"

The battle was a standoff. The Nez Perce escaped but suffered terrible losses, including some of their best leaders and warriors, Five Wounds and Rainbow among them. Joseph's wife was wounded seriously; one observer said that he had seen Joseph, when the battle was young, carrying his baby daughter to safety.

The Nez Perce turned a running battle into flight. No one among them, except Joseph, believed any longer that the whites would let them live in peace.

They crossed into Wyoming, captured a party of tourists in what is now Yellowstone Park, let most of them go with wild stories to tell, then turned back into Montana.

Now the end was in sight.

* * * * *

The Nez Perce stopped for rest on the slopes of the Bearpaw Mountains in northern Montana. Canada, and safety from the pursuing bluecoats, was no more than a day's march away.

On the last day of September in the year 1877, Colonel Nelson Miles of the Fifth Cavalry, U. S. Army, sighted the camp of the Nez Perce. He had marched from Fort Keogh, near Miles City, Montana, to prevent the final indignity — the escape of the Nez Perce into Canada. Colonel Miles ordered an attack.

Surprised, drained of energy by two and one-half months and about 1700 miles of gruelling travel and frequent battle, the Nez Perce began the final encounter with two strikes against them.

The women and children and the old ones scattered into the hills. The first storm of high-country winter chose this moment to begin to move in.

Several Nez Perce leaders, including Joseph, escaped the first cavalry charge. But Ollokot, Joseph's brother and leader of the young braves, was killed, and so was Toohoolhoolzote.

Joseph was caught unarmed and far from camp. He flung himself on a horse and raced toward his tent through a shower of bullets. His wife gave him his rifle, saying, "Here is your weapon. Fight!"

The first rush of the cavalry was stopped as the Nez Perce, drawing on their last reserves of energy, fought back.

Disappointed in his hopes for a quick victory, Colonel Miles decided to lay siege to the Nez Perce village; he hauled up his artillery and began to fire into the camp.

The Nez Perce dug trenches to protect themselves from the exploding shells. A cavalry charge which would have cut off the Indians from their water supply was rebuffed but the artillery took a terrible toll of Nez Perce.

Joseph fought like a man possessed, in spite of the gnawing knowledge that somewhere in the storm were his wife and baby daughter, stripped of protection from the snarling wind.

The battle raged into a second day, then into a third, and the storm became a blizzard.

Then General Howard, running madly in pursuit of his reputation, arrived with reinforcements.

The Nez Perce spirit was finally broken. Joseph knew that further resistance would result only in extermination of his people. The promise of the Sioux chieftain, Sitting Bull, to bring help from Canada had not been fulfilled. There was no choice now but surrender.

* * * * *

The interpreter chosen by General Howard was a treaty Nez Perce named Captain John, who had served the United States Army as a scout-interpreter. This Indian approached the headquarters of Chief Joseph on the morning of October 5, 1877.

Joseph spoke to his few remaining chiefs, and to Captain John, and through the interpreter, to General Howard and the United States of America.

"Tell General Howard I know his heart. What he told me before I have in my heart. I am tired of fighting. Our chiefs are killed. Looking Glass is dead. Toohoolhoolzote is dead. It is the young men who say yes and no. He who led on the young men is dead. It is cold and we have no blankets. The little children are freezing to death. My people, some of them, have run away to the hills and have no blankets, no food; no one knows where they are — perhaps freezing to death. I want to have time to look for

Joseph's surren

inted by Remington

my children and see how many of them I can find. Maybe I shall find them among the dead.

"Hear me, my chiefs, I am tired. My heart is sick and sad. From where the sun now stands, I will fight no more forever."

It is said that Captain John, the treaty Indian, delivered Joseph's message to General Howard with tears in his eyes.

Several hours later, Chief Joseph of the Nez Perce, with five warriors murmuring at his side, rode up the hill toward the camp of General Howard, dismounted and handed over his rifle, then drew his bullet-tattered blanket over his face, as an humiliated warrior would, and shuffled slowly into a tent of the enemy.

One of the last tribes had been shattered; one of the last great chiefs had surrendered. The long fight of the Indians against white invaders had ended.

* * * * *

In the years to come, the remaining Nez Perce were shuffled around the country like cattle, first to the Dakotas, then to Oklahoma. They sickened and died on unfamiliar ground, in strange climates.

But white protests, fanned into flame by many magazine and newspaper articles, brought Joseph and the Nez Perce back to the Northwest in 1885. They were settled on the Colville Reservation in eastern Washington.

Joseph tried many times to be transferred permanently to the Land of Winding Waters, with his people. He was always refused; he died in 1904 on the Colville Reservation. He was buried at Nespelem, Washington. A white doctor said that he died of a broken heart. Perhaps this was a poetic exaggeration; Joseph tended to inspire poetry.

Only once did Joseph return to his beloved Wallowa Lake area. This was in 1900. When he saw that a white friend had fenced and cared for the grave of his father, Joseph wept.

After Joseph died, many friends, white and red, attempted to return his remains to the Wallowa country. They failed.

Joseph's bones remain at Nespelem.

* * * * *

In his later years of life, Joseph gave an interview which was published in the "North American Review" for April, 1879. Listen

60

Joseph in later years

to Joseph, as his words come ringing down the years and echoing through the halls of troubled modern America:

"I know that my race must change. We cannot hold our own with white men as we are. We only ask an even chance to live as other men live. We ask to be recognized as men. We ask that the same law shall work alike on all men. If the Indian breaks the law, punish him by the law. If the white man breaks the law, punish him also.

"Let me be a free man — free to travel, free to stop, free to work, free to trade where I choose, free to choose my own teachers, free to follow the religion of my fathers, free to think and talk and act for myself — and I will obey every law, or submit to the penalty.

"Whenever the white man treats the Indian as they treat each other, then we shall have no more wars. We shall be alike — brothers of one father and one mother, with one sky above us and one country around us, and one government for all. Then the Great Spirit Chief who rules above will smile upon this land, and send rain to wash out the bloody spots made by brothers' hands upon the face of the earth. For this time the Indian race is waiting and praying. I hope that no more groans of wounded men will ever go to the ear of the Great Spirit Chief above, and that all people may be one people..."

Joseph has spoken.

THE BACKGROUND

In the state of Washington is one of the largest monuments ever built to honor an American Indian, Chief Joseph Dam on the Columbia River about forty miles southwest of Joseph's grave.

But Oregon, too, remembers the great Indian it spawned. The town of Joseph, in Oregon's northeastern corner, carries his name. Near the town and close to Wallowa Lake is the grave of Joseph's father. The Wallowa country is still much as it was when Joseph and his father lived there. It is not hard to see, even today, why they loved it.

The town of Joseph recalls the days of its Indian hero annually with a summer festival called "Chief Joseph Days." A mountain in Wallowa County — and perhaps the most fitting monument of all — was named "Chief Joseph" in 1925.

There is even a breed of horse to remind modern Oregonians

Joseph's grave at Nespelem

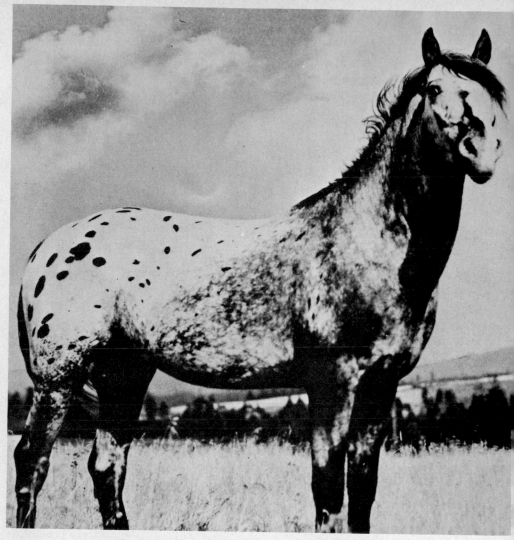

An Appaloosa, originally bred by Nez Perce

of Joseph and the Nez Perce. Called "Appaloosa," it is a strong and strikingly handsome saddle animal with wild spots and blotches of color. The intelligent, animal-wise Nez Perce developed the breed.

But there were many other Indian tribes, and parts of tribes, in Oregon when Lewis and Clark first saw the land. Estimates range as high as 40. Most of them lived in small bands scattered about the state.

The early Oregon attitude about Indians was not much different from that of the rest of the country. This feeling is expressed rather well in newspaper clippings, like this one from the Portland "Oregonian" in 1863:

"A party of miners have returned to Owyhee from a raid on Indians with twenty scalps and some plunder. The miners are all well."

And, from another newspaper of the time: "A band of Indians is camped near town. It is not known if they are peaceful or hostile. Kill them all and let the Lord select his own."

George W. Riddle writes graphically of the white attitude toward the Cow Creek Indians of southern Douglas County:

"In the four years after 1851 their numbers had diminished over half. The sources of their food supply had been greatly diminished by the settlers' fields and livestock, especially hogs, that ravaged their camas fields. Many of their race had been ruthlessly killed. In 1852 a young Indian, a son of Chief 'Wartahoo,' was hung at the William Weaver place. It was claimed that he had insulted a young white woman... within four hours he was hung...

"At another time one of our young Indians went south with a pack train, and leaving the train, was on his way home when he was stopped by white men that were at a trading post on Wolf Creek... there was a chance to have some fun by hanging an Indian, so the boy was placed upon a horse, a rope was put around his neck and attached to a limb of a tree. At this point in the proceedings, the proprietor of the house, Dr. ...., rushed out, crying, 'Hold on, that Indian owes me six bits.' The hanging was delayed until the Indian produced the money and paid his debt... When these business matters were concluded the horse was driven from under the boy and the hanging was completed. When the facts of this affair became known that trading post was given the name of the 'Six Bit House' by which it was known afterwards...

"Some of my readers may conclude that my sympathies were with the Indians and insofar as the unjustifiable outrages committed upon a helpless, ignorant people are concerned, I am content to be termed an Indian sympathizer, and I am safe in saying that ninety out of one hundred of the actual settlers — the home builders of the early days of Oregon — were disposed to treat the Indians fairly. There were numerous other persons, especially in the mining districts, that looked upon the Indian as having no rights that a white man need respect. These men called themselves 'exterminators.' Right-minded people called them 'desperados.' "

The names of Oregon's old Indian bands ring musically on modern ears. There were the Kalapooyans, who occupied most of the Willamette Valley before the coming of the whites; the Chinookans, who lived along the south bank of the Columbia from the Cascades to the ocean; the Umatillahs, Teninos and Tyighs, who inhabited the highlands of eastern Oregon; and Cayuse, bands of which lived east of the Cascades and caused no end of trouble for the whites.

Names of other tribes can still be found on Oregon maps: Clackamas, Yamhill, Santiam, Umpqua, Siuslaw, Tillamook, Siletz, Klamath, Chetco, Molalla.

One of the tribes, the Chinookan, is remembered for "Chinook jargon," a language developed along the Columbia to make trading easier. The jargon was based on Chinook, with just enough English, French and common sense intermixed to make it fascinating.

Consider these words from Chinook jargon and their English definitions: "klootchman" - woman; "glease" - grease; "kwah-tah" - a quarter; "hoolhool" - mouse; "chikchik" - wagon; "chikamin" - money; "la gome" - gum; "la peep" - a tobacco pipe; "lum-rum" - whiskey; "moosmoos" - cattle; "pusspuss" - cat; "piupiu" - stink; "potlatch" - gift; "tumtum" - heart; "toh" - spitting; "skookum" - strong; "siskiyou" - bob-tailed horse; "tiktik" - a watch; "ticky" - to love.

It is not difficult to understand why such a sensible language caught on in the old days and is still remembered.

Oddly, the Indian chief most remembered in Oregon place names is Paulina, a Paiute. By white standards, Paulina was little more than a cattle-rustling, settler-murdering trouble-maker. During the 1860's in central Oregon, his name was much on the tongues of ranchers and homesteaders who lived in continual fear of Indian attack.

In the spring of 1867, two ranchers, Howard Maupin and James Clark, came upon Paulina and a band of Paiutes breakfasting on a stolen steer. Maupin and Clark opened fire. The Indians fled but Paulina fell with a bullet in his hip. Paulina suffered even the final indignity: Maupin took his scalp.

No noble speeches came from Paulina's lips, no masterly retreats did he engineer, no glorious last stands did he make. Nevertheless, in Oregon today there are the Paulina Mountains south of Bend, Paulina Lake, Paulina Creek, Paulina Peak, Paulina Prairie and a town called Paulina.

Is it possible that white settlers were more willing to be reminded of what happened to Paulina than of what happened to Joseph? Is it possible that we see here the scars of guilt in a generation of Oregonians which tried hard to convince itself that the only good Indian was a dead one?

In southern Oregon, east of the Cascade Mountains, before the white man arrived, the Modocs and Klamaths ruled. It was the Modocs who gave to history the chieftain best remembered after Chief Joseph. His name was Captain Jack.

Captain Jack's problems — and the problems of his Modoc people — were much like those of Joseph and the Nez Perce; the pressure of white settlement was squeezing them to death. But Captain Jack was not Joseph; he was less of a statesman than Joseph and more of a hothead.

Captain Jack made the one great mistake which Joseph never made: He lifted a pistol during a peace parley with the whites and shot General E. R. S. Canby of the United States Cavalry through the head.

This angry act cost Captain Jack his life. He was hanged in 1873, but not before he led his Modocs through one of the epic chapters in Oregon Indian history, the long, bloody fight in the lava beds south of Klamath Falls.

The place where Captain Jack and the Modocs fought, on the Oregon-California border, is now a national monument.

Today the Indian population of Oregon rests at about 13,500. Approximately 2500 live on reservation lands held in trust by the Bureau of Indian Affairs of the U. S. Department of Interior. There are two Indian reservations in the state, Warm Springs and Umatilla; the Burns Paiute Indians live on public domain land.

SUGGESTED READING

Cochran, George M.; INDIAN PORTRAITS OF THE PACIFIC NORTHWEST; Binfords & Mort; 1959.

Daugherty, James; MARCUS AND NARCISSA WHITMAN; Viking; 1953.

Davis, Russell, and Ashabranner, Brent; CHIEF JOSEPH: WAR CHIEF OF THE NEZ PERCE; Whittlesey House; 1962.

Johnson, Jalmar; BUILDERS OF THE NORTHWEST; Dodd, Mead; 1963.

Miller, Helen Markley; THUNDER ROLLING: THE STORY OF CHIEF JOSEPH; Putnam's; 1959.

Porter, C. Fayne; OUR INDIAN HERITAGE; Chilton; 1964.

Scott, Paul and Beryl; ELIZA AND THE INDIAN WAR PONY; Lothrop, Lee and Shepherd; 1961.

Wood, Elizabeth Lambert; MANY HORSES; Binfords and Mort; 1953.

CHAPTER FIVE – Mining:
JOYFUL JACKSONVILLE

Mining camps in the old West were usually rowdy and full of beans. Big money was made in a hurry; big money was often spent in a hurry. In the process, everybody seemed to have a lot of just plain fun. If one gold pocket petered out, there always seemed to be another just over the ridge. If the flour supply threatened to run short, bake not bread; bake apple pie.

It was like this in southern Oregon's Jacksonville, after gold was discovered in 1852 . . .

It remained like that in Jacksonville until Oregon's biggest bonanza faded into history half a century later. It can be said even today that the town attracts a special type of person more given to fun and frolic than to the dull, workaday pursuits of more sober, less imaginative citizens.

It is fitting that this should be so. If old Jacksonville life seemed hopelessly unrefined and carefree to starchy inhabitants of Portland, the typical citizen of Jacksonville couldn't have cared less.

Yes, Jacksonville had its own way of doing almost anything.

Such as welcoming the President of the United States . . .

Rutherford Birchard Hayes, 19th President of the United States, came to town in 1881. He lived to regret it.

The only place suitable for a president in the town was the magnificent United States Hotel, then nearly new. The hotel was operated by a certain Madame Holt, who considered the building the crowning glory of her colorful career. She had always wanted to own a hotel. With the directness of her French ancestors, she had achieved it by marrying the town brickmason, who then promptly built the hotel. (The special Jacksonville manner again.)

President Hayes had a delightful time ... up to a point. Madame Holt welcomed him with proper ceremony, established him in her finest suite and then smiled as he made the rounds of the town lapping up the admiration of his Republican admirers. He attended a fancy ball; he met miners by the hundreds; he also met cowhands, gamblers and probably a gunslinger or two. Finally he retired to his suite in the United States Hotel.

In the morning, a crowd gathered on California Street to watch the President's departure. Among them was Madame Holt, clutching a piece of paper.

Instead of shaking the President's hand, as many others had done, she handed the President's aide a bill for one night's lodging in the United States Hotel — over $100!

The President's aide stared popeyed at the bill, then snapped, "Madam, you misunderstand. I don't want to BUY your hotel."

"Mon Dieu!" cried Madame Holt, lapsing into French. "That was a veree fine room! We go to much trouble, much expense! Zee wallpaper, zee carpeting, zee furniture!"

"And zee bill," grumbled the aide.

Two versions exist of what happened next. In one version, the aide paid the bill, mumbling all the while. In the second, the aide paid $25 and Madame Holt wrote many letters to Washington in the months that followed in an attempt to collect the remainder.

There is no doubt, though, about what President Hayes, a Republican, wrote in his memoirs concerning his stay in Jacksonville. He said that he had not minded spending his evening in town with local supporters of his political party. However, he did object strenuously to spending the remainder of the night with the entire Democratic Party — the army of bedbugs which had joined him in the presidential suite.

History does not report the comment of Madame Holt, although one can imagine.

Even solemn churches weren't exempt from the Jacksonville way of doing things. The Presbyterians hurried the completion of their church at the corner of Sixth and California streets because a wedding was scheduled. It was quite an affair, with only one small flaw.

70

Early Jacksonville

When the guests rose to leave, bustles and trousers stuck to the pews. It seems that the varnish wasn't quite dry.

There was an interesting wedding in the Methodist church, too. As the bride started her solemn walk down the aisle, her pet dogs entered the church and chased the shattered woman toward the altar, doing all sorts of damage to the lace which trailed her.

This might not have been so serious except for the fact that the organist had brought her poodle. The poodle leaped toward the intruding dogs...

Repairs were needed. The wedding was delayed for a time.

Yes, Jacksonville had its own way of doing almost everything...

There is something about gold that sets men's minds to reeling. It happened in Jacksonville, too. Between 1853 and 1880, more than $31,000,000 in gold dust passed through the little bank operated by C. C. Beekman, southern Oregon's pioneer banker.

There was more gold in and around Jacksonville than you could shake a shovel at. So anxious were the miners to get at the

C. C. Beekman and his pioneer bank in Jacksonville

lovely stuff that they undermined the town. It is hard to walk any-where in Jacksonville today without crossing an old mine tunnel.

Gold was everywhere. On one occasion, a sensitive Jackson-ville miner was accused of being stingy. He angrily took out a poke containing $700 in gold dust, ran out of the saloon and scattered the gold in the street like a farmer planting wheat.

In the morning, men went out into that street, collected the dirt and panned it for gold. So the story goes...

Everybody in Jacksonville mined gold in the heyday of the camp. They tell the story of two prisoners in the town jail who missed a meal because their jailer was out working his claim. In the Jacksonville way, the prisoners decided to tunnel out through the dirt floor of their cell. In the process, they struck gold. When the prisoner's terms were up, the jailer couldn't understand why they didn't want to leave.

Finally they agreed to go, considerably wealthier than when they arrived.

Yes, there was a special way of living in Jacksonville.

As the town grew and took on polish, dirty, red-shirted miners discovered they couldn't compete in society against swells wear-ing starched shirts and flossy vests. So some of the miners bought these get-ups, too. It was not unusual for a miner leaving Jack-sonville for a time to lend his fancy garments to a friend, who then cut his own wide swath in local society.

On one dull holiday, a band of soldiers bent on celebration loaded a huge cannon with everything imaginable and fired it down California Street. The explosion broke every window in town and cracked a few walls, too. Nobody complained too loudly. This, after all, was Jacksonville.

Jacksonville had its troubles and tragedies, too. The residents endured hunger, Indian attacks, fires, floods and smallpox epi-demics, good times and lean, but they always seemed to come through with the Jacksonville spirit undamaged.

The winter of 1853 was especially difficult for the residents of Jacksonville. Salt was particularly scarce. Sharing a pinch of salt then earned a friend for life.

Thirty years later, when an old timer gave a gift to a friend and the friend tried to pay him, the old timer said, "How could I take from a friend who divided salt with me in '53?"

This, too, was the way of life in Jacksonville...

One trouble with early Jacksonville was that it was confused. The residents weren't even sure whether they lived in Oregon or California ... and as we modern folks can testify, you can't get more confused than that.

The miners of those days were drifters. They went where the gold was. When they voted in elections, they cast ballots in whatever town they happened to be in on Election Day. The trouble was that they didn't want to pay taxes in either Oregon or California.

Whenever a representative of the Oregon Territory called in Jacksonville, the miners were Californians. When a California tax man called, the miners were Oregonians. This could only lead to confusion, which exists to this day. (A northern California weather forecast sent out by the federal government is more likely to be accurate for Jacksonville than a western Oregon forecast.)

It was not until the decade of the 1850's was well along that the Oregonians of Jacksonville decided they didn't want to be Californians, after all. Even then, though, there was a meeting in the Robinson House at which both the Jacksonville residents and their California friends tried to form a new territory called "Jackson." The movement failed. But it is a tribute to the Jacksonville spirit that to this day, occasional meetings occur in which good-natured citizens attempt to form a "State of Jefferson," during which they speak of rebellion, secession and revolt.

The fun-and-games spirit apparently infected the younger generation, too. As the town grew, railroad service was provided to Medford five miles away. The weak-lunged locomotive usually managed to reach Medford on time; it was a downhill drag. A passenger returning to Jacksonville, though, could not be sure that he would reach the mining camp on time ... or if he would reach it at all without walking part of the way. It seems that Jacksonville schoolchildren discovered that if they greased the tracks at a certain point, the boredom of a school day could be relieved by watching through schoolhouse windows as the train, its locomotive chuffing madly, slid backwards toward Medford.

The Jacksonville of today, of course, is not the Jacksonville of old. It remains, however, the best preserved of any historic community in the state. Many of the old buildings have crumbled and have been replaced by modern structures; others have been

U. S. Hotel, Jacksonville, before restoration

remodelled and restored; a few of them are much as they were in the early days.

Only recently the Urban Renewal Agency of the Federal Housing and Home Finance Agency of the United States government offered a thumping amount of money to restore old Jacksonville. (That extra thump may have been President Rutherford Birchard Hayes turning over in his grave.)

While the buildings may have suffered through the years, the mood and flavor of the old town can still be felt. A modern Oregonian in the right frame of mind can walk today along the edges of its tree-lined streets (there aren't many sidewalks) and sense the past. Rounding a corner, he might encounter a horse-drawn stagecoach. (You may, if you wish, ride that coach on a tour of the town.)

Seven buildings form the core of the new-old Jacksonville. Most prominent is the museum which occupies both floors of the old brick courthouse, a sturdy structure built in 1883-84 which

75

looks as if it might withstand another 80 years of tourist traffic. A smaller building north of the courthouse contains more relics; two other buildings on the courthouse grounds are used for display of old wagons, fire equipment, and the like. The Jacksonville museum is not, and never will be, the largest historical museum on the West Coast but it may well be one of the most interesting and best-tended.

On California Street, the United States Hotel still stands. In January, 1965, the Jacksonville branch of the United States National Bank was opened on its ground floor.

On the corner across the street from the U. S. National Bank is the historic Beekman Bank, a small building furnished as it was while in use. (The Beekman Bank never offered the "complete service" of a modern bank; it existed merely to buy and sell the golden treasure which poured out of the Jacksonville mines.) The home of C. C. Beekman is a Jacksonville showplace and museum.

A recent addition to the Jacksonville scene is the Peter Britt Music Festival, which is held each summer during the famous Shakespearean Festival at neighboring Ashland. The Britt Festival takes place on the grounds of the home of Peter Britt, Jacksonville's pioneer photographer.

No visitor to Jacksonville should overlook the old cemetery on a high point west of town. Here, amid the graves of the old timers, is where the past is most likely to seem real.

THE BACKGROUND

The diggings in and around Jacksonville were far and away the richest in Oregon. The figure of 30 millions of dollars has a mellow ring even today; it was nothing less than a bonanza in terms of the fat 19th century dollar.

Between 1856 and 1880, 5438 mining locations were registered in Jackson County. Of these, 16 were for copper, one tin, 124 cinnabar. All the rest were for gold and silver. The Jacksonville district recorded the most claims: 1463.

Mining in both Jackson and Josephine Counties continued into the twentieth century. On a much smaller scale, it is being done today. Small but dedicated groups of miners like the Josephine County Sourdoughs still work claims back in the mountains and agitate for a raise in the fixed price of gold: $35 per ounce.

Gold mining in Oregon generally fell into two categories: "placer" or "hardrock." Placer mining was far the most common

Bill Sample pans Jackson Creek near Jacksonville

method. This type of mining is based on one simple fact: gold is much heavier than any of the earth substances which surround it. The most primitive method of placer mining is panning. A miner simply puts gold-bearing earth in a pan, adds water, sloshes the mixture around until the heavy gold has had a chance to settle to the bottom, then lets the other material slop over the edges of the pan. If he is skillful enough (and lucky enough), some gold will remain in the pan's bottom.

Panning is profitable only where the earth is rich in gold. By panning, a miner could work through only a small amount of dirt per day. The "rocker" was developed to increase production. A rocker looks much like a baby's cradle; dirt was shoveled in and water was added as the cradle was rocked, allowing the worthless dirt to pass over the sides while the heavy gold flakes settled to the bottom.

The rocker was an improvement over the pan but the "sluice box" was better than either. A sluice box is a long trough with small cleats fixed at intervals along its bottom. A continuous stream of water is run into one end of the box, then pay dirt is shovelled in. As the water washes away the worthless dirt, the gold sinks to the bottom of the box and is caught by the cleats. Sometimes mercury (quicksilver), which clings to gold, was placed along the cleats to collect the precious mineral.

Hardrock mining had to be used where the gold was not loose but was encased in quartz. The quartz was dynamited or broken with a pick. Then the rock was hauled to a stamp mill, where giant hammers smashed it into small bits. As you can imagine, the sound of a big stamp mill at work was enough to wake the dead. Once crushed, the ore was processed either as in placer mining, or chemicals were used to retrieve the gold.

Finally, when most of the rich diggings had played out, hydraulic mining and dredges came into use. Great streams of high-pressure water were sent through hoses and directed against whole hillsides. The earth was washed down to giant sluices, where gold was extracted. Dredges were installed in the stream beds to suck up great quantities of gold-bearing material, which were processed on the dredge. The gold was taken out and the waste material, called "tailings," was spewed from the dredge and left in huge piles along the streams. Piles of tailings left by hydraulic mining and dredges are a common sight along Oregon's gold streams. Mass production in gold mining has left its ugly mark.

Modern hydraulic mining in Josephine County

In all of these processes, great amounts of water were used and miners went to great lengths to bring the precious liquid to pay dirt. There is a record of a ditch 136 miles long in Baker County which was hand-dug, mostly by Chinese labor, in order to carry water to the diggings. Gold production varied sharply from year to year, depending upon rainfall. In dry years, there often wasn't enough water to do the job.

A trick known as "highgrading" fattened the purse of many a hired miner. It was almost impossible to keep a man from slipping a little gold from a sluice box into a secret place when the boss wasn't looking . . . and the boss couldn't be looking all the time.

The labor of immigrant Chinese was very important in the Oregon gold fields, as it was elsewhere. Chinese often worked for as little as 25 cents a day.

Their labor was welcome but the Chinese themselves never attained great popularity. They seemed too "different." Almost every western mining community had its Chinatown, complete with joss houses (churches) and opium dens. Many Chinese workers sent their earnings back to China; many returned to China when they had amassed enough money. Some, however, remained to become respected American citizens.

Perhaps the feeling of the white miner toward the Chinese is best expressed by a Jacksonville yarn. A white miner was hailed into court for shooting and killing a Chinese. He was fined $25 for "discharging a firearm within the city limits."

Trying to avoid trouble, Chinese sometimes took over a claim after it had been abandoned by white miners and worked out what gold had been left. One might say they were the scavengers of the gold fields.

A Chinese who took his own claim and worked it profitably was Gin Lin, a familiar figure around Jacksonville in the heyday of the southern Oregon gold rush. He had come to the Jacksonville area as the boss of a Chinese labor crew, then branched out with a claim of his own in the Little Applegate district southeast of Jacksonville. Gin Lin finally went back to China to retire but he shouldn't have; the story goes that he had hardly stepped off a ship in his homeland before being killed and robbed.

Southern Oregon was not the only gold source in the state. In Grant County south of John Day, 8 million dollars' worth of gold was mined between 1862-1872. Canyon City originally was

Portland's Chinatown about 1900

a gold camp. Somewhere in this area lies the famous lost Blue Bucket mine, supposedly discovered by children of a wagon train which passed through the area. Prospectors looking for the Blue Bucket made the strike on Whiskey Flat, north of Canyon City, which triggered eastern Oregon's gold rush. At the peak, 10,000 miners and camp followers stormed through the area.

Mineral production today is not a major factor in Oregon's economy but all of Oregon's 36 counties report some output. Nationally, Oregon ranks only 38th in mineral production. From gold to oil, though, Oregon has it. Leases for oil drilling on 800,000 acres off the Oregon coast give promise of a new source of fuel and wealth. During World War II, nickel production from mines near Riddle, in Douglas County, was of great importance to the war effort.

Think of mining in Oregon, though, and you have to think of Jacksonville...

SUGGESTED READING

Hult, Ruby El; LOST MINES AND TREASURES OF THE PACIFIC NORTHWEST; Binfords & Mort; 1957.

Johnson, Jalmar; BUILDERS OF THE NORTHWEST; Dodd, Mead; 1963.

Lockley, Fred; OREGON'S YESTERDAYS; Knickerbocker; 1928.

Early Canyon City

CHAPTER SIX – Agriculture:
LITTLE MAN, BIG POWER

"Pete French is dead!"

A cowboy named Dave Crow gasped out the words, then sank exhausted to a bench. He had ridden for two days and two nights from the Blitzen Valley of southeastern Oregon to bring the electrifying news to the cattle town of Winnemucca, Nevada, in December of 1897.

Pete French is dead.

The word spread like wind lashed fire in dry grass, crackling around Oregon and the West by word of mouth, by letter, by telegraph. As the message reached Burns, where French was a frequent visitor, and Portland, where he was already a legendary figure, and Red Bluff, California, near where he was born, the first reaction seemed to be that the fabulous P Ranch had been swallowed up.

But why? A small man, hardly larger than a healthy boy, had died; nothing more. The 200,000-acre sweep of lush range land was still there; the bawling hordes of cattle, horses and mules were still there; the sturdy buildings and fences, the irrigation canals — all were still there.

But Pete French was suddenly missing, cut down in the prime of his tempestuous life by an angry sodbuster's bullet. He was the blue-steel link which held the chain together. The P Ranch was Pete French; everyone seemed to sense immediately that the ranch had to die with the man.

There were many who did not weep. These were the persons in Oregon and elsewhere who thought of Pete French as a ruthless pirate who would connive, steal or murder to protect his vast cattle empire.

But there were others, including many of those closest to him while he lived, who considered French a generous man, driven hard by ambition but usually reasonable, often kind.

Those who had worked for him, many of them range-toughened Mexican cowboys called "vaqueros," swore by him and gave easily the loyalty he demanded. Those who had blocked the path of his enormous ambitions, like the homesteaders around Malheur and Harney Lakes, had reason to fear and hate him.

Pete French had lived and worked in southeastern Oregon for 25 years before his sudden end. This was enough time for a small but head-strong and heart-strong man to build a cattle empire and a legend. Pete French was such a man.

He had come to southeastern Oregon as a young man in 1872, driving a herd of about a thousand cattle. His backer was Dr. Hugh J. Glenn, who had built a beef empire near Red Bluff, California, and had taught young French much of what he knew about turning cattle into dollars; it was considerable.

French was not the first cattleman who had seen the possibilities of this empty land. Men like John Devine and Peter Stenger had come before. But luck took a hand in leaving the long and rippled valley of the Donner und Blitzen River for Pete French. A number of unusually wet years had occurred before French's arrival. Water slopped over from the Blitzen and soaked the surrounding meadows. Devine and Stenger left the Blitzen alone; it looked to them like permanent swamp, not cattle range.

French's first impression was quite different; to him, the Blitzen Valley seemed to offer the raw materials for the cattle kingdom he intended to build.

The Donner und Blitzen River pours out of the Steens Mountains at a wild clip, then flows quietly along a valley thirty miles long and five miles wide, picks up the trickle of many little streams as it progresses, and empties into Malheur Lake. It was a land that a steer could roam for many months of each year, whetting its appetite on the thick lowland grasses through spring and early summer, then moving into the snow-watered highlands as the dry season parched the bottoms. In the process, that steer would grow fat for the Winnemucca market.

French moved in and went to work. Along the way, he had bought the "P" brand from a discouraged cattleman. Now he set about building P Ranch. French was not a hit-and-run operator;

he built like a man who had come to Oregon to stay. Strong juniper formed his corrals and buildings. (He built so well that a few of those early buildings still stand.) Bunkhouses and cabins were thrown up for his vaqueros; stone walls fenced the canyons; juniper posts and smooth wire marked his advancing empire to anyone who had notions of intruding. Canals spread grass-growing water through the lowlands.

He brought in more cowboys. The work was hard and the hours long but they were well-paid by the standards of the time, and their families were well-housed and well-fed. No job as big as P Ranch became could be a one-man operation; there needed to be dozens of others who cared about its success or failure. Pete French picked the men and Pete French made them feel like working. Runt and pirate he may have been but fool he was not; he knew better than most employers what makes the garden grow.

The mold of his life in Oregon was set.

And the mold of his death, as well...

* * * * *

The life and personality of Pete French formed the pattern for a character called "cattle baron" in a thousand Western novels, in hundred of Western movies and now in many more television epics based on material gleaned from the days of the open range.

But the real Pete French could not have played the part in books or in movies and television. At his tallest, he never stretched over five feet, six inches, and he was outweighed at his heaviest by any yearling calf in his herd. Many a muscular vaquero on his payroll could have grabbed him by the seat of his saddle-worn pants and thrown him into the nearest juniper tree.

But if anyone ever tried this stunt, history does not record it.

His hard-gray eyes, his small but rock-solid body, his skill with fist and gun, his knowledge of cattle and horses and men, discouraged such Sunday afternoon tricks. All of these qualities had to be part of Pete French, or he could not have turned a far-flung wilderness into a cattle kingdom.

He was the kind of employer who seldom asked an employee to do work that he wasn't willing to do himself. What's more, little Pete probably could do that work better. The work was often dangerous, as well as hard, and French assumed his share of the risks, as well... often more than his share.

86

Pete French

There was the time, for instance, only five years after French had settled into the Blitzen, when the Paiute and Bannock Indians grew restless and angry under the increasing pressures of white settlement. The Indians knew what had happened to Joseph and the Nez Perce during the previous year; the Paiutes and Bannocks had no reason to believe that they would fare any better. They also were inspired by the knowledge that Joseph had won many victories. Perhaps the white soldier, after all, was only a paper tiger.

As French and his crew worked the ranch during the summer of 1878, rumors of Indian uprising drifted on the wind. Trouble struck directly at French as he and a crew of about 16 men were branding calves at Diamond Ranch, part of the French holdings in the Blitzen Valley.

A settler named Sylvester Smith had come to the Diamond from Happy Valley, ten miles away, to borrow running gear for a wagon. He stayed at the Diamond overnight, then set out for home early on July 14 with his team and wheels.

As Smith prepared to leave, French warned with a small smile, "Mr. Smith, if Buffalo Horn tries to beg a ride, you just wave nice, whistle something pretty and keep your team a-movin'."

Smith snorted, took a swipe at his nose, and said, "Mr. French, that Bannock won't have no trouble atall with me, on account of I don't plan to let him get that close. Much obliged for the wheels. See you next week."

But Sylvester Smith was going to see the P Ranch boss much sooner than next week.

As the homesteader neared the summit of the grade leading out of the valley, he pulled up, squinted and felt a nervous sweat break out on his weathered face.

A party of more than 20 Indians, Bannocks by the look of them, sat horses just beyond the big gate in the stone walls which French had used to fence the rimrock.

A quick glance at the war paint sported by the Indians was all Smith needed to prod him into action. He jumped down immediately, cut the traces from the faster of the two work horses, then leaped onto its back, bellowing and whacking the animal's flanks. He knew that his chances were slim of outrunning sleek Bannock ponies but a slim chance was better than none. He forced the animal to do its lumbering best in a desperate dash toward the Diamond Ranch buildings.

Then luck, in the form of a sturdy French gate, took a hand.

The mechanism of the gate was strange to the Bannocks. For several moments, they were unable to open it. Finally, after some angry wrestling with the gate, the Indians whooped through and set out after Sylvester Smith.

The delay had given the homesteader all the advantage he needed. His horse carried him into the ranch yard well ahead of the pursuing Bannocks.

"Mr. French!" roared Smith. "Remember them Indians we was talkin' about? I brung a few!"

Pete French's White House

French and the cowboys had been saddling up in preparation for the day's work when Smith plunged into the yard.

"Saddle up faster than you ever did before!" ordered French as he reached for the rifle. "Chico, don't forget to saddle one for the Chinaman! Then ride out pronto! I'll hold 'em off!"

The cowboys obeyed with frantic haste as the first onrushing Bannocks stormed into view and bore down on the scurrying group. Moving with the speed of a hungry cat, French leaped onto a gate, shielded his thin body behind a thick juniper gatepost, then opened fire on the leading Bannocks.

He dropped one quickly, then another, causing the Indians to pull up in billowing dust and scatter into the protecting rocks.

The Bannocks soon spotted their tormenter on the gate. Leading their horses, half a dozen warriors climbed a rocky slope in order to draw a bead on French. The delay was long enough to allow the crew, including Sylvester Smith and the Chinese cook, to ride out for the safety of P Ranch headquarters.

French continued to trigger a deadly barrage. When he saw that his crew had ridden safely out of range, the P Ranch boss leaped to the back of his horse and rode in pursuit of the vaqueros. Glancing over his shoulder, French saw flames leap from a Diamond ranch building, then from another. Diamond was being burned out, but Diamond's boss could do nothing but gallop away from his smoking property.

French soon caught up with his fleeing crew who had turned up McCoy Creek. The leading Bannocks quickly narrowed the gap; arrows and bullets began to sing a deadly song in the ears of the French cowboys as they fled up the creek bed.

Then the Chinese cook, not much of a horseman, fell from his mount and sprawled in the dirt; his horse clattered up the creek bed. The cook's loss was Sylvester Smith's gain. Smith's work horse, already tired when Smith left the ranch yard, had fallen back. When the cook's mount with an empty saddle caught up, Smith grabbed the bridle, leaped into the saddle and set out after French and his cowboys.

The Chinese cook died; Bannocks found him later, hiding in the brush.

The safety of the ranch house was still more than a mile away from the fleeing French crew and the Bannocks were narrowing the gap, their bullets and arrows coming ever closer to their targets. The cowboy's horses were beginning to stumble with fatigue.

French glanced back at the pursuing warriors as his crew neared the rocky bluff which now loomed as the last barrier between them and safety. He realized immediately that his men would be spotted like ducks in a shooting gallery as they struggled upward on their weary mounts.

French spurred his lathered horse. The animal stretched its neck and burned its last bit of energy as it leaped ahead of the group and clambered toward the crest of the ridge.

The horse reached the summit. French leaped down, fell to one knee and began to work his rifle. The P Ranch crew labored up the ridge; the Bannocks turned loose a deadly fire at slow-moving targets.

One Bannock fell under a French bullet, then another, and still one more.

The war chief of the Bannocks, who knew how death could spread from a good gun on high ground, halted his warriors with a shout and a raised hand. The Bannock fusillade fell off; the French crew reached the ridge but not before a cowboy, John "Ochoco" Witzel, had felt in his hip the impact of a Bannock bullet. Soon the entire French crew, including Witzel, was throwing lead at the Indians.

The Indians were ordered to retreat. The tide had turned; death for many brave Bannocks glowered down from the ridge.

The chief, on this fateful day, had other fish to fry. He held a brief council, then turned away toward Silver Lake to join Chief Egan and the Paiutes, who also were out to make trouble for whites during this bitter time.

The French crew was safe for the moment. More Indian trouble was to come in the weeks and months ahead. P Ranch cowboys, and French himself, would play a major part in the fighting which threatened for a time most of Oregon's white settlers.

But as the Bannocks rode off, the immediate danger ended for P Ranch and its men.

The legend of Pete French, however, was just beginning.

Even those who called him a conniving pirate and a land thief

91

could now understand why he always had the loyalty of those who knew him best — his cowboys.

*****

Indian trouble, to Pete French and his California sponsor, Dr. Glenn, was only an episode, another obstacle to be conquered. Most of the hostile bands were quickly wiped out or placed on reservations. The work went ahead on P Ranch. Great tracts of land were added as range for more cattle; borders of the ranch were thrust into the far distance. Land, by the thousands of acres, was bought, leased and — some say — stolen.

It was a good time for Pete French. The White House at P Ranch headquarters was the scene of much entertaining as the little cattleman tried to strengthen his hold on the Blitzen. But the land changed with the changing times. An obstacle no larger than a homesteader's shack popped up...and mighty Pete French stumbled over it.

Much of the prime farming land in Oregon's Willamette Valley had already been homesteaded. Latecoming settlers, spurred by reports of new "dry-farming" methods, brought their wagons and their families into the Blitzen Valley, put up shacks and sod houses and squatted on land which Pete French and other ranchers considered their own.

Like French, the homesteaders were hungry for land; riches were in the earth. It seemed to the homesteaders that Pete French had laid claim to most of the world. Surely, they thought, this was wrong.

Farming, homesteader style, and cattle ranching, Pete French style, could not co-exist. Trouble soon developed. Brave or foolish homesteaders nibbled at P Ranch boundaries.

Pete French had come to the Blitzen to stay. This was his home and his empire. It was cattle land, it was his land, and nobody — Bannocks, homesteaders or law officers — was going to drive him from it.

He decided to fight to hold the Blitzen if it killed him.

It killed him on the first day after Christmas.

*****

Among the homesteaders in the Blitzen Valley lived an obstinate man named Ed Oliver. Oliver had moved into the swamplands around Malheur Lake and had fenced his property with

Pete French's round barn

barbed wire, which Pete French hated.

On Christmas Day, 1897, French had returned from a business trip to the East. He rode a buckboard out from Burns toward the ranch. The next morning, he discovered that a cattle drive foreman, Chino Berdugo, was sick. In his characteristic way, French sent Berdugo to the ranch house and took over preparations for the drive.

On a cold winter day, French approached a gate on the ranch. Ed Oliver galloped out of the sagebrush and rode hard toward French. The horses struck each other. According to the cowboy who was closest to the action, French struck at Oliver with a whip to fend him off, then turned to ride away.

Oliver fired.

Pete French fell from the saddle, killed by a bullet which had ripped through his head.

Oliver galloped off. P Ranch hands covered French's body with blankets, then, as night fell, erected a tent over his remains. A P Ranch cowboy guarded the tent through the long night which followed.

French was 48 years old when he died; he had been 23 when he first saw the Blitzen Valley. A sharp-nosed bookkeeper said that he died a rich man; his net worth was about two million dollars. But his money was no protection against Ed Oliver's bullet.

At least half a dozen men had seen Ed Oliver kill Pete French. Nevertheless, at the Harney County courthouse in Burns a few months later, Oliver was acquitted of the murder charge and set free. A jury had spoken; twelve good men and true had found Oliver innocent. To this day, you mention the trial of Pete French in Harney County only at the risk of starting an argument.

A reader of history must wonder if that Harney County jury really tried Ed Oliver ... or merely made a judgment on the life of Pete French.

THE BACKGROUND

One wonders how Pete French would feel if he could know that the land which saw so much feuding during his lifetime is now a peaceful haven for thousands of migratory birds.

One wonders, too, what the little cattle baron would say if he could know that most of the homesteaders who fought him

Malheur National Wildlife Refuge

so bitterly were starved out of the Blitzen Valley not long after his death. It was not dry-farming country after all; the homesteaders might as well have left it to the cattlemen.

In 1908, only 11 years after French's death, the Malheur National Wildlife Refuge was established around Malheur and Harney Lakes. In 1935, 65,717 acres were sold to the federal government for an addition to the Refuge. Almost all of this latter tract was once owned by Pete French and Dr. Glenn. It was sold to the government by Swift & Company, a very large meat packing concern. Even as mighty an organization as Swift had not been able to earn a profit from a cattle operation along the Blitzen.

Apparently this piece of earth needed a man like Pete French ... and it lost him too soon.

But there were others besides Pete French who tried to establish southeastern Oregon as stockman's country: John Devine and Peter Stenger have been mentioned earlier. One other was Henry Miller, who took a back seat only to French. There were Colonel James Hardin and William W. "Wagontire" Brown. (Brown was primarily a sheep man.) William Hanley was another. It was Hanley who took over management of P Ranch after French was killed.

These men and others built the livestock industry in eastern Oregon. Today this industry remains a major one east of the Cascade Mountains. Range wars, however, are only a sad chapter from the past. Much of the grazing land today, a vast 13 million acres of it, is owned by the public and leased to stockmen.

The center of the livestock industry in Oregon has moved north from Pete French country to the Bend-Redmond-Prineville area and east to Pendleton, LaGrande and Baker, where wheat, Oregon's major crop, also occupies an important place.

But Pete French left his mark. Several of French's barns, including the famous Round Barn, still stand. One can forgive the absence of a few shingles; after all, the winds of many years have sighed over the grave of the little baron of the Blitzen.

Near Frenchglen, at what once was P Ranch headquarters, is the site of French's home, the renowned White House. The house burned but the chimney still stands.

Pete French was buried in Oak Hill Cemetery in Red Bluff, California. He started from Red Bluff and there his trail ended.

Curious antelope at Malheur National Wildlife Refuge

The small town of Frenchglen in Harney County honors his name. Frenchglen and Burns, seat of Harney County, are the jumping-off places for the thousands of persons who visit the Malheur National Wildlife Refuge each year.

On the land in Oregon where Pete French made his mark on history, in the places where his great herds used to graze, clouds of migratory birds now wing down through the peaceful air to nest each summer.

The birdwatchers know their names — ducks and geese, pelicans and cranes, terns and gulls, egrets and herons. A few species, such as the sandhill cranes and trumpeter swans, might have perished forever if this place had not been set aside for them.

Where once raged the frightening sounds of white man fighting red man and cattleman fighting homesteader, we now may hear, if we care to listen, the mating cries of birds in a shelter provided by man.

Trumpeter swans at Malheur National Wildlife Refuge

Early day apple harvest near Hood River

A person inclined toward poetry might see in that simple fact some hope for the human race.

* * * * *

For crop farming, Oregon's Willamette Valley offers some rather special conditions. It is hardly surprising then that Oregon's agricultural strength, after wheat and barley, is in specialty crops. Seed growing gets particular emphasis. No place in the world, for instance, grows more ryegrass seed than Oregon.

In 1970, Oregon ranked first in the United States in production of snap beans, filberts, winter pears, sweet cherries, blackberries, black raspberries, loganberries, Boysenberries, youngberries, peppermint, processing strawberries and several seed crops. Oregon is known throughout the country for its bulbs and other nursery products.

Growing farm produce is no longer enough; processing to preserve it for shipment and sale has become increasingly important. Many Oregonians will be surprised to learn that the second largest canning and freezing center in the United States is in Oregon at Salem, where great quantities of fruits, vegetables and berries are processed each year.

The suffering of Oregon's early settlers along the long trail was made easier to bear by the storied promise of fertile, well-watered valleys which awaited them along the Willamette. Modern production figures indicate plainly that the promise has been fulfilled.

SUGGESTED READING

Johnson, Jalmar; BUILDERS OF THE NORTHWEST; Dodd, Mead; 1963.

Powers, Alfred; TRUE ADVENTURES ON WESTWARD TRAILS; Little Brown; 1954.

CHAPTER SEVEN – The Women:
GIANTS IN PETTICOATS

She was a tough little lady, was Abigail Scott Duniway.

But anyone who called her this in her day would have been wise to accent "lady." Otherwise he might have felt the lash of her sharp and active tongue.

But when a woman of her time set her mind to do what she did, it wasn't enough to be a lady; she had to be as tough as any man and on many occasions, even tougher.

Once as she spoke in the mining camp of Jacksonville, eggs were thrown at her. (There is no record as to whether the eggs were fresh or otherwise. Knowing the crude manners of many of the men who inhabited Jacksonville, though, one could safely guess otherwise.)

She was attacked bitterly in the newspapers of Oregon as a man-hater, even though she loved and was loved by a good husband, five sons and a daughter.

She was slandered as a woman of loose morals by politicians in public meetings and even by ministers speaking from their pulpits. Over her long career, she received many letters which attacked her for this reason and others.

Many of her enemies accused her of taking bribes from liquor interests, which at that time were waging a war against a surging swell of prohibition sentiment around the country. The same accusation was made by some of her supposed friends and co-workers.

At various times she was barred from churches in Oregon and elsewhere. She suffered cruel abuse from the very group to which she had devoted the work of her life, the women of Oregon and America.

101

Why?

What terrible thing did this woman want which brought such brutality down upon her head?

The answer is simple — she merely wanted women to have the right to vote.

The word in those days for this right was "suffrage." The word is outmoded now; it has an old-fashioned air, like "buggy" and "butter churn." But it was a word which was very much in the minds of most Oregonians and most Americans during the last half of the nineteenth century and during the opening quarter of the twentieth.

The right to vote now is taken for granted by all young women and most older women. But in the time of Abigail Scott Duniway, this right seemed a distant dream. Only many years of dedicated labor by thousands of women made the right a reality in Oregon and the United States. Only the fanatic efforts of a handful of talented, energetic and downright stubborn leaders, fighting against terrible handicaps, gave women the right to vote.

In the forefront of these leaders was Oregon's Abigail Scott Duniway.

She was a tough lady who lived to see her dream realized...

* * * * *

The suffrage fight was long and hard for a number of reasons. Most obvious, though, was this one: Since only men could vote, there could be no equal suffrage laws on the books unless the votes of men put them there.

This sort of unequal battle needed women with enough fighting spirit to gain the respect of men, yet with enough womanly charm to avoid setting male voters permanently against women and their cause. This is by no means a common combination of qualities, but Abigail Scott Duniway had it.

She replied to the egg-throwers of Jacksonville by referring scornfully to such a tactic as a "Jacksonville argument." She called the egg-throwers "Missouri bushwhackers."

It must have been the proper approach, because in time Jacksonville became a stronghold of pro-suffrage sentiment.

She replied to the newspaper attacks with tart editorials in her own newspaper, "The New Northwest," which she published

Mrs. Duniway (center) casts her first vote

weekly in Portland. The best answer to the cries of "man-hater" was the obvious fondness she felt for her own largely-male family. Those who attacked her as a woman of low morals eventually were smothered in their own lies; they were made to look foolish as many more persons came to know the honest, upright woman who was Mrs. Duniway.

Those who accused her of taking money from liquor interests were never able to make the charge stick. This accusation grew out of Mrs. Duniway's determined efforts to separate the cause of women's suffrage from prohibition. She was afraid that many men feared a vote for suffrage was, in effect, a vote for prohibition of liquor. Even the national leader, Susan B. Anthony, mightiest suffragette of them all, failed to recognize this. Eventually Mrs. Duniway was proved to be entirely correct in taking this stand.

Some of the ministers who had barred her from their churches eventually became her supporters and welcomed her; perhaps her own strong religious feelings became plain enough in time to win them over.

She was a hard-driving, impatient woman, was Abigail, but she could also be enormously patient in waiting for the right moment to reply to an attack.

On one St. Valentine's Day, her husband, Ben C. Duniway, brought home a large envelope containing a valentine for his wife. She opened it to discover a sheet of poster-sized paper on which was pictured a hen-pecked husband trembling in terror. Clambering over the man were a batch of yowling children. Above his frightened form stood a toothless, straggling-haired woman, threatening him with a broom. Under the picture was the verse:

"Fiend, devil's imp, or what you will,
  You surely your poor man will kill,
  With luckless days and sleepless nights,
  Haranguing him with Woman's Rights!"

Humiliation crushed Abigail. "Did I ever give you, or anybody else, a reason for attacking me with a thing like this?" she asked tearfully.

"No. It was sent by some fool as a joke. If I'd known what it was, or that you would care a rap about it, I wouldn't have brought it home."

Years later, Abigail Scott Duniway was presiding at a suffrage meeting in the opera house at Salem on St. Valentine's Day. Some cruel wit sent a large envelope to the platform. Mrs. Duniway opened it; it was the same bitter valentine of years before, showing the same browbeaten man.

She advanced to the front of the platform and displayed the valentine to the audience.

Then she said, "The author of this exquisite piece of art didn't give his name, but he has sent along his picture."

Yes, she was a tough lady, whom you attacked at your own peril.

The man-hater charge was one to which she had to reply constantly, both in speeches and in print. One of her strongest responses came during a speech before a convention of the National American Woman Suffrage Association at Grand Rapids, Michigan, in 1899. Addressing herself to men, she said:

"We are glad to be assured that you 'love women,' but we are doubly glad to be able, on proper occasions, and in every suitable way, to return the compliment. No good Equal Suffragist will any longer permit you to monopolize all the pretty speeches about the other sex. Every good woman in the world likes men a great deal better than she likes women, and there isn't a wise woman in all this goodly land who isn't proud to say so. We like you, gentlemen, and you cannot help it. We couldn't help it if we would; we wouldn't help it if we could. You like us, also, because you cannot help it. God made the sexes to match each other. Show me a woman who doesn't like men, and I will show you a sour-souled, vinegar-visaged specimen of unfortunate femininity, who owes the world an apology for living in it at all; and the very best thing she could do for her country, provided she had a country, would be to steal away and die, in the company of the man who doesn't like women . . . "

On another occasion, she addressed a woman's rights meeting in Gervais. When she had finished, a young, impertinent lawyer of the community delivered a sarcastic speech in reply. Finally, after half an hour, he folded his arms dramatically, puffed out his chest and proclaimed, "In conclusion, gentlemen, allow me to say that I have often known a hen to try to crow, but I've never known one to succeed at it yet!"

The young man took his seat amid laughter and applause. Mrs. Duniway laughed as heartily as anyone, then rose to reply.

"Friends," she said, folding her arms and imitating the pompous tones of the young lawyer, "I am almost ashamed to notice the last clause of my friend's argument, but I must not forget that I am here to demolish, if I can, the sort of opposition that has been set up ... I am free to confess that the gentleman is right; I have discovered myself the same peculiarity in hens. But in the poultry yard of my friend, Colonel D. M. Thompson of Albany, I once saw a rooster try to set, and he made a failure, too!"

The young lawyer slipped quickly out of the hall.

This was not the only barb that she planted. Once she was travelling by stagecoach through central Washington between Goldendale and Yakima. Snow was falling, the day was cold and there was a biting wind. As was so often the case, she was the only woman in the coach. One of the male passengers grew bored and bold and chided Mrs. Duniway, finally saying, "Madam, you ought to be at home, enjoying yourself, like my wife is doing. I want to bear all the hardship of life myself, and let her sit by the fire, toasting her footsies."

Mrs. Duniway didn't answer ... then. It was almost dark when the stage reached Yakima. The driver, an obliging fellow, went out of his way to leave the man who had spoken to Mrs. Duniway at his own doorstep.

In the yard was his wife, wearily chopping away with an axe at a pile of snow-covered cordwood.

As the man stepped down from the coach, Mrs. Duniway cleared her throat and said, "I see, my friend, that your wife is toasting her footsies ... "

Mrs. Duniway heard later that the man developed the nickname around Yakima of "Old Footsie Toaster."

But she didn't always have to fight alone. One morning in Portland her family was seated at the breakfast table. One of her sons, Willis, had brought in a weekly newspaper. He unfolded it, glanced at the editorial page, turned pale and showed the page to his brother Hubert.

Then, without a word, the brothers rose from the table, taking the paper with them, and left.

Instinctively Mrs. Duniway knew what was wrong: She had been attacked again and her sons were responding. She followed her sons to the door and begged them not to do anything rash.

They did not answer but instead hurried away.

They didn't return until the next day, when they announced that they had been arrested for assault and battery and had been released on bail of ten thousand dollars. Bail had been furnished by a Portland businessman, D. W. Prentice.

Later, Mrs. Duniway was told by the prosecuting attorney, J. F. Caples, that he had risked his official position by telling the Duniway boys in court, "Stay with it, boys. You did exactly right!"

The newspaper in question was kept out of the mails. On Monday morning, the "Oregonian," edited by Mrs. Duniway's brother, the famous Harvey Scott, defended her vigorously in an editorial.

But Abigail was frightened, nevertheless, as she left the house on that morning to go to her office. She had held up her sons to the world as badges of her competence as a wife and mother. Now two of her sons had been arrested and charged with a serious crime. What would this do to her reputation? How badly would it hurt the suffrage movement?

She stepped into a street crowded with men, bowed her head and hurried along. She knew these men were talking about the affair and perhaps now they would abuse her for it. They could say, with some justification, that the trouble was the result of a mother's neglect; if she had only stayed at home instead of rampaging around the country trying to turn women into men ...

Lifting her head, she recognized J. N. Dolph, later to be a United States Senator from Oregon. He crossed the street to her and she stiffened against the expected rebuke.

But, in the middle of the street, Mr. Dolph lifted his hat and when he neared, offered his hand!

Suddenly every man in the crowd removed his hat and stood bareheaded as Abigail Scott Duniway went weeping by.

She was a tough lady, was Abigail, but she knew how to cry ...

* * * * *

The issue, of course, was never simply that of earning the right of women to vote. The vote was merely a means to an end. The end was a new life for the women of America, a new life free from the harsh treadmill of child-bearing, child-rearing, life-sapping physical drudgery which was the lot of most women in the nineteenth century. It was not a problem which existed only in Oregon; the sickness covered the nation from Oregon to Maine, from Florida to California.

Abigail Scott Duniway, as a young girl in 1852, travelled the Oregon Trail with her family from Illinois to the lush pastures of the Willamette Valley. But her mother never saw Oregon. Already weakened by overwork, child-bearing and illness, she died of cholera along the trail in what is now Wyoming. It is likely that in the grief-torn moment of her mother's burial, the cast of Abigail's life was formed.

In Oregon, Abigail married Ben C. Duniway and bent her back alongside his to carve out farms in Clackamas and Yamhill counties. Her husband was a good man, kind and hardworking, but he was a creature of his times.

In those times, women could not legally own property . . . but they could be held responsible for their husband's mistakes in property-buying. Women could not legally take on a debt . . . but they were responsible for the debts of their husbands. Women could not serve on juries and carried no weight in a court of law . . . but they were expected to obey the laws which men had made.

The Yamhill County farm was lost when a debt contracted by her husband could not be met. Abigail considered this a tragedy at the time, although she saw it later as a release from bondage. It was followed by another tragedy; her husband suffered an injury which prevented him from working. It fell upon her to make a living for a growing family.

She rose to the occasion. She kept a boarding house. She taught school. She operated a millinery. Somehow she kept her family afloat. Finally, with the advice and encouragement of her brother, Harvey Scott, she started a suffrage newspaper and called it "The New Northwest."

But it was her kind and loving husband who first showed her the way to a better life for women. She had been telling him of the latest incident involving a woman who was drowning in an ocean of trouble created by men, run by the laws of men.

"One-half of the women are dolls," she raged. "The rest of them are drudges . . . and we're all fools!"

Ben Duniway put his hand gently on his wife's head. "Don't you know it will never be any better for women until they have the right to vote?"

"What good would that do?" asked Abigail.

"Can't you see that women do half of the work of the world? And don't you know that if women were voters there would soon be lawmakers among them? And don't you see that, as women do half the work of the world, besides bearing all the children, they ought to control fully half of the pay?"

In that moment, in the year 1870, a leader of women was born.

In 1872, the first law was enacted by the Oregon legislature recognizing the legal existence of married women. It was called "The Married Woman's Sole Trader's Bill." A law empowering women to vote for school trustees and funds was passed in 1878.

Then, after many failures, a law empowering women to vote in Oregon was approved by a proclamation of Governor Oswald West on November 30, 1912.

In an historic gesture, Governor West asked Abigail Scott Duniway of Portland to write the proclamation in her own hand, which she did. By this time, she was old and ailing and could not go to Salem to watch the governor sign the proclamation.

So the governor came to her...

The Oregon territorial motto was: "She flies with her own wings."

Surely that motto pleased Mrs. Duniway immensely.

A reporter from the "Oregonian" sought her out at her home two days after the election which brought suffrage to the women of Oregon and final victory to Abigail Scott Duniway. He found her seated in a rocking chair with a pillow behind her head. On a table were scores of letters and telegrams of congratulation.

The reporter was surprised that she did not seem excited, only contented and peaceful; he mentioned his surprise.

"I knew it would come now," she said serenely, "but had it by any chance been delayed, we had made arrangements whereby the fight could be renewed at once."

She was a lady, was Abigail Scott Duniway, a tough lady...

THE BACKGROUND

The Oregon Trail, they said back East in the 1840's, was a harsh and difficult road even for a strong young man who had money to spend. Yet, in 1846, a person came over this trail who was 66 years old, who weighed little more than a hundred pounds, who was crippled by paralysis of one leg and who arrived in Oregon with a total wealth of six and one-quarter cents.

Remarkable? Add the fact that this person was able to found a university in Oregon and it becomes unbelievable. Then add the fact that this person was a woman in a day when women were allowed to be little more than household drudges and it becomes impossible.

Yet a woman accomplished this in Oregon. Her name was Tabitha Brown. The school she founded at Forest Grove in Washington County exists today as Pacific University.

A widow, Mrs. Brown left her Missouri home in April, 1846, in a wagon train which included her son Orus and his family, plus her brother-in-law, Captain John Brown, 77 years old. After a relatively easy trip to Fort Hall in what is now Idaho, the train split. Convinced by glowing promises of a new southern route into the Willamette Valley which avoided the hazards of both Mt. Hood and the Columbia River passage, the Browns joined a party which set out to enter the Promised Land through the Rogue and Umpqua Valleys of southern Oregon.

They experienced great difficulty; the party split into many smaller groups. Finally, in the Umpqua Valley near present-day Roseburg, the old man and the crippled woman found themselves alone, struggling northward threatened by Indians, sickness and starvation. By this time, wagons of the party had been destroyed or abandoned and they slogged forward on weary horses. Captain Brown became delirious and barely able to sit his horse; once dismounted, he was too weak to get back into the saddle.

Tabitha, using two canes as props, somehow lifted him back into the saddle.

Captain Brown lived to reach Salem and safety on Christmas Day of 1846. It is quite likely that a little old lady, Tabitha Brown, wasting no energy on tears and refusing to give in to exhaustion, made it possible.

She found a small coin called a "picayune," worth six and one-fourth cents, in the finger of her glove. With the coin, she bought large needles, then traded old clothes to Indians for buckskin, from which she made gloves for sale. By spring, her capital had grown to $30.

Tabitha Brown was on her way...

Mary Walker

She started a small school for orphans at West Tualatin Plains, which is now known as Forest Grove. Working night and day, charging only those students who could afford to pay, she made the school prosper. Once known as Tualatin Academy, it is now officially Pacific University.

Tabitha Brown died at age 78 in Salem and took an honored place in the history of Oregon women. A monument at Pacific University commemorates her; a building at the school is named after her.

Wives of missionaries who came West intending to convert Indians to Christianity made the first female imprint on Oregon history. Among these were Anna Lee, wife of Jason Lee; Narcissa Whitman, the beautiful young wife of Dr. Marcus Whitman; Eliza Spaulding, wife of Henry Spaulding; and Mary Walker, an intelligent, outspoken woman who was married to Elkanah Walker, a missionary to the Spokane Indians, who later transferred to Forest Grove. Of this group, Mary Walker was outstanding as

111

an example of the kind of courageous, thoughtful and stubborn woman who was soon to demand her place in a male world, but Narcissa Whitman is much better known, perhaps only because she died violently in the famous Whitman Massacre.

There were other women who left deep footprints in Oregon. One such was Bethenia Owens, a bright, headstrong young lady who became Oregon's first fully-qualified woman doctor. She started her practice in Roseburg, where she had operated a millinery store, and succeeded in shocking the frontier town to its boots. Eventually she moved to Portland, where she was attacked, ridiculed and defamed. She lived, however, to see some of her most rabid opponents become her supporters and admirers.

The strain of hardy, productive womanhood in Oregon has not run thin over the years. Consider the example of Emma Carstens McKinney of Hillsboro, publisher since 1904 of the state's most-honored small town newspaper, the "Hillsboro Argus." She remained active in publication of the "Argus" until illness forced her retirement in 1962.

She won in 1957 the highest honor available to an Oregon newspaper person, the Amos Voorhies Award. She is the only woman ever to be so honored. In 1949, she was named as an Oregon "Woman of Achievement" by the Portland alumnae chapter of Theta Sigma Chi, professional journalism sorority. In 1958, Oregon Press Women decided to begin awarding an "Emmy" to the outstanding newspaperwoman in the state, honoring Mrs. McKinney through use of one of her nicknames. Over the years, the "Argus" has won 37 national awards for journalistic excellence. Her son W. Verne and two grandsons are engaged actively in carrying on the tradition established by Emma C. McKinney.

Abigail Scott Duniway would have been delighted with Oregon's 1965 delegation to the United States Congress. Two of the six members were women, Senator Maurine B. Neuberger and Representative Edith Green. Both have served with distinction, the former since 1960 and the latter since 1954. Only two women in the United States had been elected to a full term in the U. S. Senate before Senator Neuberger.

Mrs. Green was only the second woman to be sent to the U. S. House of Representatives from Oregon. Nan Wood Honeyman, elected in 1936, was the first.

Portland's first woman mayor, Dorothy McCullough Lee, was placed in office in 1949.

Perhaps because Oregon provided so much to write about, many of Oregon's outstanding women made important marks as writers. Frances Fuller Victor is a proud early literary name. In 1870, she wrote "The River of the West," a biography of Joe Meek. She followed in 1872 with "All Over Oregon and Washington" and in 1893, she was authorized by the legislature to compile a history of the early Oregon Indian wars.

Another early writer of note was Eva Emery Dye, who came to Oregon in 1890 and settled at Oregon City, where she listened with fascination as her neighbors told stories about Dr. McLoughlin. Her first book was "McLoughlin and Old Oregon," published at the turn of the century. It is still one of the most popular books dealing with Oregon history.

Frances Fuller Victor

Among those Oregon women who are now writing books for a national audience are Victoria Case, Evelyn Sibley Lampman, Martha Ferguson McKeown and Eloise Jarvis McGraw.

And so times have changed for women in Oregon, as elsewhere. The life of the pioneer woman has been glamorized but in truth, it was hard and frustrating, with death usually ending it early. It is even more remarkable then, that Oregon's history should be sprinkled with the names of outstanding women. Or perhaps it isn't remarkable at all. Hardship breeds giants; a very special kind of woman could lift her head above the crowd.

This was the kind of woman who thrived on discouragement, who loved nothing more than the challenge of a worthwhile fight against overwhelming odds.

When Dr. Bethenia Owens had won her battle, a woman from Roseburg who had once condemned her came to Dr. Owens in Portland for medical treatment. The woman approached her former enemy with fear and trembling.

Dr. Owens surprised the woman by clasping her hand and thanking her for putting obstacles in the path of that headstrong Roseburg girl named Owens who once had the foolish notion of becoming a physician.

"You see," said Bethenia to the surprised woman, "a friend once said to me, 'If I wished to increase your height two and a half inches, I would attempt to press you down, and you would grow upward from sheer resentment.'"

They say that you can't keep a good man down. In Oregon, the saying seems to apply to women, too.

SUGGESTED READING

Johnson, Jalmar; BUILDERS OF THE NORTHWEST; Dodd, Mead; 1963.

Miller, Helen Markley; WESTERING WOMEN; Doubleday; 1961.

Ross, Nancy Wilson; HEROINES OF THE EARLY WEST; Random House; 1960.

Wolfe, Louis; ADVENTURES ON HORSEBACK; Dodd, Mead; 1954.

CHAPTER EIGHT – Modern Government:
THE LAWGIVER

The young man stepped into the dirty little office. While he waited for the attention of the bald man seated at a rolltop desk in the corner, he examined the political posters tacked on the grimy walls. His eyes didn't see the dirt; they saw only the Republican candidates as they stared somberly down at him from the gaudy posters. He felt his excitement grow as he waited amid the bustle. This was politics and he was more sure than ever that politics was what he wanted.

The young man was William S. U'Ren; the place was Denver, Colorado; the year 1880. The bald man was a boss of the Republican Party in Denver. U'Ren had heard that the Republicans were looking for help.

"He'll see you now," said a smiling lady in a flowered hat.

"Thank you, ma'am." U'Ren edged toward the corner desk.

"Sir," he began nervously, "my name is U'Ren. I heard — "

"What? What was that name again?"

"U'Ren. Here ... I'll write it for you."

He grabbed a piece of paper out of a wastebasket and carefully wrote: "William Simon U'Ren."

The bald man looked at it, then sniffed, "Funny name."

Despite his nervousness, the young man grinned. "It is, rather, I'll admit."

"You the man Goodrich sent? He a friend of yours?"

"He's my landlord. He said the Republicans were looking for volunteers, so I — "

"All right. We need a man in the seventh precinct. You know that part of town?"

"A little."

"Good," the bald man said. "It's tight over there. Could go either for us or against us. So we're colonizing."

U'Ren blinked. "Pardon me?"

"Colonizing. We're shipping in Republicans to tip it our way. See Mrs. Carmody by the front door. She'll tell you what to do."

"But, sir...is that legal? I mean...can you have people vote who don't live there?"

The bald man stared at U'Ren for a long moment. "I forgot. You're new. Young man, we'll worry about what's legal after we win the election."

"I...I see. To tell you the truth, sir, I'd rather do some other kind of work."

The bald man stared at the ceiling for a time, then leaned forward and said quietly, "U'Ren...or whatever your name is... around here I say who does what. That's politics. You don't want politics. You want the Ladies' Aid."

Disappointed and angry, U'Ren left the office and walked the streets of Denver. After an hour of walking, he was attracted to an ugly murmur which rose on a side street. He hurried to the corner.

Down the street marched a mob of men carrying banners and placards. One banner screamed: "Send the Chinks back to China!" Another one echoed: "Chinese must go!" A number of placards carried a harsh message: "Kill Chinamen!" Another cried: "America for Americans!"

As the mob passed, with its members bellowing threats against all Chinese, a brick flew out of the group and crashed through a store window. The mob turned to look, then roared with laughter.

The mob passed out of sight and soon out of hearing. Young U'Ren was shocked. Purposefully he strode back to the Republican Party office and boldly confronted the bald man at the corner desk.

"Maybe I can work for the Republicans after all," announced U'Ren. "Did you see that mob? If the opposition party won't help those poor Chinese, the Republicans ought to!"

116

The bald man let his jaw hang for a moment, then smiled. "U'Ren, you're right. I hereby appoint you my deputy. Go protect those Chinamen in the name of the Republican Party."

"Thank you, sir," said U'Ren eagerly. "I'll do my best. This is the kind of work I wanted to do!"

For three days U'Ren made speeches to anyone who would listen, wrote letters to the newspapers and stirred up all the support he could for the much-abused Chinese, always remembering to point out that he was acting as an official of the Republican Party.

One evening as he came home wearily to his rented room he met his landlord on the front step. U'Ren sat beside him and spilled out the full account of his hard work.

Finally Goodrich put his hand on U'Ren's shoulder and shook his head. "Bill . . . don't feel too sorry for those poor Chinese."

U'Ren frowned. "But . . . why not, Mr. Goodrich? Haven't you seen those terrible mobs marching the streets, destroying property and — "

"Bill, believe me now. I know the Republican Party in Denver a whole lot better than you do. Most of the men in those mobs are good Republicans."

"What!"

"Certainly. They don't hate Chinamen any more than you or I do. But if they can get enough of our good citizens worried about mob rule, those good citizens will come out on Election Day and vote for the party of law and order — the Republican Party. Understand?"

William U'Ren understood. For the second time in his young life, he had come face to face with a political truth. He had thought he might some day go to the United States Congress. Now that dream vanished. He wanted no part of such a dirty business.

But a new dream took shape. He realized that the most important work he could do might be to make laws which would make such crude shenanigans more difficult and less profitable.

His life was set in Denver in a direction which was to lead him to a secure position in Oregon history as William U'Ren, the lawgiver. It was a direction which was to make Oregon very special in the eyes of the United States as a pioneer force in legislation for democratic government and for the good of mankind.

117

William S. U'Ren

He came to Oregon in 1890. It was almost accidental that he remained; it was a lucky accident for Oregon.

He arrived afire with a new idea for taking government away from the political bosses and giving it back to the people. The idea was called "initiative and referendum," or simply "I. & R."

Here, at last, was the tool William S. U'Ren had been looking for...

* * * * *

What were initiative and referendum?

Essentially they were simple. Initiative makes it possible for the people to make laws, whether or not their elected representatives approve of those laws. Referendum makes it possible for the people to repeal laws whether or not elected representatives approve.

In other words, it made political bosses of the people. With "I. & R.," the people could start or stop any legislation by voting directly for or against it. The system would make legislators responsible to the voters at large, rather than to any special group with an axe to grind.

Initiative and referendum were first used extensively in Switzerland. In 1890, when U'Ren decided to make Oregon his home, such a system was badly needed all over the United States.

At that time, the government in Oregon was very corrupt. Powerful interests such as railroad companies bought and sold legislators as if they were high-priced cattle. (Ben Holladay was a master at this.) In fact, political corruption in Oregon had become so common that it was almost respectable. Old documents prove that some of Oregon's most esteemed citizens were involved in the vote-buying. Even U'Ren himself, in trying to correct the evil through I. & R., was forced occasionally to resort to methods of which he was not at all proud.

U'Ren met E. W. Bingham in Portland. Bingham gave a piece of advice to use in working with political organizations.

"Never be president," advised Bingham. "Get a president and a committee; let them go to the front. The worker must work behind them out of sight. Be secretary."

U'Ren never forgot the advice. He always was secretary when he worked with a group and remained behind the scenes... but busy. (This policy may have cost him his rightful place in history; little has been written about U'Ren, either in Oregon or elsewhere.)

But those who wanted information from the many committees on which U'Ren worked soon learned where to go for it — to U'Ren.

The first legislative campaign in Oregon involving U'Ren brought the Australian, or secret, ballot to the state. Bingham helped; they made a good team. U'Ren was smooth and smart; Bingham was a blustering bulldog.

Thus started in public service, U'Ren still had to think of making a living. He was taken into partnership by a group of nurserymen and orchardists in Milwaukie, all of whom were as interested in good government as U'Ren. They read; they studied; they talked; they thought.

The partnership broke up in 1893 after a bitter argument but, characteristically, U'Ren said later that his health, his heart and his mind all were better for his years among the Luellings of Milwaukie.

U'Ren joined the Populist Party. Populists, by and large, were reformers, sincere people who wanted to change government for the better. Soon U'Ren was secretary of the Populist state committee. Before long, he had maneuvered the initiative and referendum plank into the Populist platform.

Then U'Ren went to the people. As secretary of the Direct Legislation League, he wrote a brochure explaining initiative and referendum.

He got much help. Women put the brochures together. It was said that the work went on feverishly in two-thirds of the homes in Milwaukie during the winter of 1893-94. They prepared 50,000 folders in English and 18,000 in German. Other groups, including labor unions, saw to it that the brochures were distributed and read.

The campaign worked. When politicians said to U'Ren that they knew nothing about initiative and referendum and hence couldn't possibly vote for it, U'Ren could reply softly, "The people know about them."

But U'Ren wasn't satisfied. He went to Salem as a lobbyist for the people and buttonholed every one of the legislators at one time or another.

Despite the corruption of the legislature, he squeezed out promises of "yes" votes from a solid majority of the men he talked to.

But when the moment of truth arrived with the vote in both houses of the legislature, initiative and referendum lost...

It lost by one vote in the House of Representatives. It lost by one vote in the Senate. U'Ren claimed that the bill lost in the Senate by one wink from the president of the Senate — Joe Simon, political boss of Portland.

U'Ren recovered from his disappointment and went back to work for the people of Oregon. The fight for initiative and referendum continued.

In 1898, U'Ren said to a friend, "I am going to get the initiative and referendum in Oregon if it costs me my soul. I'll do nothing selfish, dishonest, or dishonorable, but I'll trade off parties, offices, bills — anything for that."

After eight years of work, U'Ren had become a real power in Oregon; he had become a man who was listened to at all levels of government. In 1899, he was ready to try again.

He and his co-workers made new friends in the legislature and kept a close watch on their old ones. He went so far as to tell legislators that he didn't really believe in initiative and referendum; he said that he agreed with them in thinking that it was a "crank" measure. He continued to back it, he said, only because his Populist supporters demanded it.

"What does I. & R. amount to, anyway?" he would say. "It has to be approved in two sessions of the legislature. Pass it now and the Populists will be happy. Then we can beat it in the next session and that will be the end of it."

The initiative and referendum measure came to a vote in 1899.

It passed the House, 44 to 8, and passed the Senate, 22 to 6.

U'Ren, of course, had no intention of casting aside the victory he had fought for so long. As soon as the session closed, he went to work to make it impossible for the political bosses to beat it in the next session.

His work was effective. At the next session in 1901, when the measure came up for the second vote, it was approved unanimously. At the next general election in 1902, the people approved it by an 11-1 margin.

Oregon had freed itself from the utter corruption which had poisoned its government for many years. Oregon had initiative and referendum ... and still has to this day.

The people were again in control ... and remain in control today.

In a book published in 1905, Lincoln Steffens, famous political-social writer of the day, said, "I believe that the state (of Oregon) will appear before long as the leader of reform in the United States, and if it is, W. S. U'Ren will rank in history as the greatest lawgiver of his day and country."

Steffens interviewed U'Ren at U'Ren's small home near Oregon City. Among many questions Steffens asked was this one, "How well off are you, U'Ren?"

U'Ren put down the axe with which he had been chopping firewood. "I think that I am one of the richest men in Oregon," he said, after some thought.

"How is that?" asked Steffens. "Have you made money?"

"My earnings," said U'Ren, "average about $1800 a year. But that isn't what I mean. I haven't any money, but I haven't any wants, either, not for myself."

"But what about the compromises you have made with corruption?" Steffens asked. "You may have saved the people of Oregon, but haven't you lost your own soul? What are your chances of going to heaven, do you think?"

U'Ren was staring at his hands and didn't seem to realize that Steffens was speaking half in fun.

After a long moment, U'Ren looked at Steffens and said quietly, "Well, I would even go to the other place for the people of Oregon."

THE BACKGROUND

In Oregon, as in all the American states, a man called "governor" rules the roost.

Under Oregon law, a governor must be at least 30 years old, a citizen of the United States and a state resident for at least three years before taking office. In Oregon, a governor is elected for a four-year term. He can be re-elected for another four-year term but then must take a four-year vacation before running again for the office.

Capital Mall in Salem

The governor, in addition to serving as the state's chief executive, also prepares the state budget and is commander-in-chief of the state's military forces. (As you may have guessed, this last duty doesn't demand a great deal of his time.)

He can veto bills sent to him by the legislature and can call special sessions of the legislature. He can appoint many heads of agencies, boards and commissions. He is chairman of the Board of Control and Land Board and a member of various other boards and commissions.

With all this, one is caused to wonder how a governor finds time to cut ribbons at openings of new highways; yet a highway opening without a governor's scissors can hardly be considered a highway opening at all. It is quite likely that a typical governor spends as much time on such ceremonial fol-de-rol as on the official duties of his office. Voters seem to like it that way. So do many governors, since a ribbon-cutting in some remote corner of the state provides a fine opportunity for a little political fence-mending. A governor must be a vote-getter, to be a governor at all, and tradition has it that the chief executive who spends too much time sitting in office in Salem is well on his way to becoming a former governor. Voters like to see and touch their elected officials once in a while, so travel within the state is a must for a governor. (Travel **outside** the state, however, no matter how good the reason, can be the kiss of political death, in Oregon as elsewhere. Voters and taxpayers like a chief executive who seems to be tending the store, night and day, month in and month out.)

For putting up with all this, Oregon's governor is paid $21,500 per year. He also gets an expense account, of course.

If a vacancy occurs in the governor's position, Oregon law specifies that he will be succeeded by the President of the Senate and in order, if need arises, by the Speaker of the House, Secretary of State and State Treasurer.

In addition to governor, four other top Oregon posts are filled by election: secretary of state, state treasurer, labor commissioner and attorney general.

The state legislature, consisting of the Senate and House of Representatives, is ordered by law to meet in Salem starting on the second Monday in January following each biennial election. There are 30 Senators elected for four-year terms and 60 representatives elected for two-year terms. A senator or representative in Oregon needs to be only 21 years old to qualify but to have a chance of election, he should be seven or eight years older than that and give the appearance of being at least 35. (A touch of gray hair helps, unless one happens to be a woman, in which case the political rule book can be thrown out. There is no record of a woman being handicapped in politics by youth and beauty.)

Oregon has never had a woman governor and probably won't for a good many years, unless another Abigail Scott Duniway should soon brighten the Oregon scene. Not likely; her kind comes along about once each century. She would have made a fine governor.

Although they have been denied the governor's chair, a few women usually sit in both houses of the legislature.

One of Oregon's best-remembered governors is Oswald West, who served between 1911 and 1915. We are indebted to Governor West for the fact that Oregon is unique among the coastal states in that only 25 miles of its fantastically beautiful coastline is privately owned.

In 1958, a plaque was installed at Neahkahnie Mountain in Oswald West State Park on the Oregon coast. The inscription reads: "If sight of sand and sky and sea has given respite from your daily cares, then pause to thank Oswald West, former Governor of Oregon (1911-1915). By his foresight nearly 400 miles of the ocean shore was set aside for public use from the Columbia River on the north to the California border on the south. This marker is erected and dedicated by the grateful citizens of Oregon to commemorate this outstanding achievement in the conservation of natural resources."

Governor West is remembered, too, because he served as Oregon's chief executive when woman's suffrage was finally granted in the state. It was he who asked Abigail Scott Duniway to write the proclamation which made woman's suffrage official; it was he who called at the aged lady's home in Portland to accept the proclamation.

Oregon's historic habit of leading the way in governmental experiments has carried into the present. Consider the field of civil rights, for instance. Oregon's constitution, ratified in 1857, prohibited slavery but also prohibited the entry into Oregon of free Negroes.

125

Mrs. Duniway signing Oregon's equal suffrage proclamation
with Gov. Oswald West and Mrs. Viola M. Coe

Today, however, Oregon's fair employment practices and public accomodations laws which protect the rights of minority groups have more teeth in them than the federal laws covering the same injustices.

Oregon may be backward in some respects but in the area of government, it has often been a pathbreaker.

SUGGESTED READING

Tucker, E. Bernice; YOUR GOVERNMENT IN OREGON; Harr Wagner; 1956.

CHAPTER NINE – The Railroads:
WAR IN DESCHUTES CANYON

One fine day in 1908 a fisherman appeared on the Deschutes River in north-central Oregon. Nothing was unusual about that; the swift-running Deschutes is one of Oregon's finest fishing streams.

The fisherman's name was John F. Sampson, or so he said. "Fine river you've got here," Sampson told the natives. "Fine country, too. Don't know when I've enjoyed fishing so much."

He liked the country so well, in fact, that he bought options on quite a few chunks of it. "Nice fellow," said the natives about John Sampson. "He puts his money where his mouth is."

It was not until some time later that ranchers and farmers in the area discovered that while Sampson was certainly fishing, he was not fishing for fish; he was fishing for a railroad.

Sampson played his role just long enough to buy the stock and charter of the Oregon Trunk Railroad from a man named William Nelson for $150,000. Portland's Mr. Nelson had a charter, nothing more. Until Sampson came along, the Oregon Trunk had been little more than a stock promotion scheme; it hadn't laid a foot of track.

Sampson's real name was John F. Stevens, an engineer who had just recently left a post as chief of engineers on no less a project than the Panama Canal. The $150,000 came not from his own pocket but from that of James J. Hill, often considered the most important of American railroad builders.

Thus the stage was set for the last great open-air railroad battle in the United States. It took place in Oregon, between The Dalles and Bend, during the years 1908-1910.

Nowadays railroad fights take place on the littered floors of stock exchanges and are of interest mainly to readers of the "Wall Street Journal". These modern squabbles are fought with figures on pieces of paper; the Deschutes Canyon brawl between one-eyed Jim Hill and Edward H. Harriman was fought with fists, bullets and dynamite. It ended not when the stock exchange closed but when the battlers were exhausted. They struggled not only with each other but against some of the most rugged and rocky land ever to resist railroad building, against summer heat, winter winds and rattlesnakes.

It was a battle of titans, Hill vs. Harriman, with the rich empire of Central Oregon as the stake. Both men had fought bigger battles but the fire in both was burning low; this was to be their last important struggle.

Hill, in fact, had "retired" a year before the battle of Deschutes Canyon erupted. He had stretched the Great Northern west to Seattle as the main link in his railroading empire, and had just finished an extension of his Spokane, Portland & Seattle line along the north bank of the Columbia River to Portland.

Harriman had made his mark with the historic Union Pacific, which he had driven across the West into California. Later Harriman had taken over the Southern Pacific, which is today Oregon's major north-south line.

After Ben Holladay and Henry Villard had failed in Oregon railroading, a long period of relative inactivity followed. The Harriman group had taken over but laid little new track. Great areas of Oregon still weren't served by rail lines. The natives grew restless; there was widespread grumbling against Harriman.

Jim Hill, looking down from the north, saw a chance to win a last battle from his old foe, and sent John J. Sampson fishing along the Deschutes. Once the Oregon Trunk had been bought, Hill announced that he would bridge the Columbia and build down the Deschutes to Bend.

Harriman wasn't fooled. He suspected that Bend would be only a way station on a line that Hill intended to build all the way into California, in which case it would compete directly with Harriman's Southern Pacific. True, there was a great deal of ponderosa pine in Central Oregon which a railroad could transport to market, but, farther south, there were the riches of California; Harriman knew that Hill had an eagle's vision.

Hand-built grades on both sides of Deschutes River

Harriman immediately chartered the DesChutes Railroad. Since Hill had already decided to build on the east bank of the Deschutes River, Harriman announced that his company would build on the west bank. He hired George W. Boschke, who had just finished construction of the famous sea wall at Galveston, Texas, to oversee the Central Oregon construction.

"The line of the DesChutes Railroad," said Boschke, "will parallel that of Mr. Hill from the Columbia to Bend. Or, for that matter, to anywhere else that Mr. Hill cares to go."

It was a rash statement. Nobody, not even Edward H. Harriman, could wave a red flag in the face of Jim Hill without getting butted.

And so the railroad war began...

* * * * *

One does not build a railroad merely by sending out great gangs of immigrant laborers to carve out roadbed and lay track. Much preliminary work had to be done. Maps of the proposed route had to be filed with the government; right-of-way had to be purchased; surveying was necessary. Very little of this work could be done in secret. A single John F. Sampson could wander along the Deschutes without exciting much interest but Jim Hill couldn't send a thousand Sampsons armed with picks and shovels into the area without letting the opposition know that some railroad-building was afoot.

A common trick of the day was to file for a route under a different name. In 1908, the Central Oregon Railroad informed the proper government agencies that it intended to lay rails between Madras and Bend. The maps which were filed gave Central Oregon Railroad legal rights to a certain crossing of the Crooked River.

Apparently Jim Hill had nothing to do with the Central Oregon Railroad, but in 1909, Central Oregon Railroad was bought by Oregon Trunk, Hill's little paper railroad. Now Hill had the important crossing of the Crooked River that he needed. It seems plain that a certain amount of bluffing was going on. Survey crews were sent out along the proposed route of both lines and contractors were hired, Porter Brothers by Hill and Twohy Brothers by Harriman. Supplies were brought by steamer up the Columbia, unloaded at The Dalles, then hauled south by branch line railroad and wagon into the empty land.

In the Deschutes Gorge, which was only a few hundred feet wide along much of its length, the battle began. Surveyors engaged in casual gun battles; bullets flew from one side of the gorge to the other. Either this was just more bluff or the surveyors were poor shots, because most of the bullets missed their targets.

But the pattern was set...

In midsummer of 1909, both sides announced their plans to build railroads into Bend. In short order, work camps were established on both sides of the river. The trickle of supplies through The Dalles became a flood; thousands of workman poured into the area.

The work south of The Dalles went quickly and smoothly. But in the Deschutes Gorge, a strong Hill tracklayer could lob a sharp rock into a gang of Harriman workers on the other side of the river.

Harriman's crews awoke one morning to discover that the wagon road over which their supplies were coming had been cut off. Porter Brothers, during the night, had merely moved some dirt in the right places.

With only heat and rattlesnakes to contend with, the gorge that summer would have been a miserable place to work. Adding to the torment of the laborers was the fact that this was a pick-and-shovel railroad; it was too long a haul for heavy equipment from The Dalles and besides, much of the big machinery would have been useless in the rocky gorge.

The Hill forces on the east side of the river tried to pretend that they couldn't care less about what the Harriman crowd was doing.

"We are not watching the Harriman forces," announced Johnson Porter of Porter Brothers in "The Dalles Chronicle". "We are just sawing wood and going ahead ourselves and don't care what they do...

"On the other hand, they watch us like hawks. When we want to know where to locate one of our teams, where it spent the night, etc., all we have to do is ask some of the Harriman men and they can tell us in a minute without any expense to us... While they watch us work, we go ahead and do things."

The inhabitants of Central Oregon read these remarks with great interest. The desert has always been shy on entertainment;

Tunnels and railroad grades along Deschutes River

Hill and Harriman suddenly were providing quite a lot of it. Central Oregon hadn't been so lively since the sheep-cattle wars of the 1870's.

Newspaper accounts of the time make plain that Harriman had done himself no good in Oregon by virtually stopping extension of the lines for a long period after he took over from Henry Villard. "The Dalles Chronicle" obviously favored Hill in its accounts of the struggle. This newspaper reported with glee an attempt by Harriman to buy out Porter Brothers. Said Johnson Porter in the "Chronicle": "The Harriman interests offered to give back all the money we had spent up to that time with a handsome profit thrown in and an interest in their contract besides if we would sell out to them. My reply both times was that we would not sell out for $5,000,000."

The battle raged, with one side gaining a temporary advantage, then the other.

The Twohy Brothers built a wagon road at a cost of $8000 from Grass Valley to their work site on the Deschutes, a distance of about seven miles. Porter Brothers promptly bought the property which the road crossed and put up "No Trespassing" signs.

The Harriman forces got much of their water from a spring on land owned by a certain French and Downing. Porter Brothers bought the spring, then put up a sign: "No Water to Spare. Porter Brothers."

All this was comparatively polite when judged against what was happening down at the work sites. When the day's work was done, it was not unusual for a gang from one camp to row a boat across the river for a knock-down, drag-out brawl. These nightly excursions began with "thumping and knuckle-dusting," but soon grew more serious when pick handles and rocks were hauled across the river. Almost every train back to The Dalles over the new lines carried victims of the nightly battles.

Inevitably, each side dreamed up new tricks to fill idle hours. Both crews sent spotters up onto the cliffs to peer across the river, with particular attention being paid to where dynamite was being stored. Then, on the first dark night, a few brave or foolish souls would slip across the river and set off the explosives.

Men died; those who lived often were maimed. Yet no charges of murder or criminal assault were filed; workers and bosses alike seemed to consider personal injury as just another hazard of railroad building.

Such acts would not be taken so lightly today, of course. It must be remembered that these were different times. Human life was shorter and cheaper then. If either side lost a few laborers under the blows of a pick handle, there were always more to be found. In 1909, ships in New York harbor were unloading European immigrants by the thousands and the cattle cars of Hill and Harriman were hauling them west as fast as they straggled off the docks. Common laborers earned 20 or 30 cents an hour and were glad to get it. If their employers were heartless, it must have seemed a small thing to the immigrants when laid against the opportunity they had been offered of making a new life in this large, uncrowded land.

The war along the Deschutes had reached a peak which could not be sustained. Millions of dollars had been poured into the fight. Reading the old accounts, it seems as if Hill and Harriman, the tired warriors, realized at almost the same moment that their fight along the Deschutes had been essentially a personal one, a determination on the part of each to go down in history as America's premier builder of railroads.

On May 17, 1910, a cease-fire agreement was achieved. The competing lines decided to share the rails for eleven miles along the Deschutes Canyon. Later this joint use was extended.

When the golden spike which fastened the last rail was driven in Bend on Railroad Day, October 5, 1911, James J. Hill was there to drive it. Harriman's representative was William McMurray, general passenger agent of the Union Pacific.

Like most "golden spikes," this one didn't hold a rail for long. It was pulled out and given to an old, bearded man — Jim Hill. According to Bend author Phil Brogan, Hill gave the spike to Bill Hanley, the cattleman who took over P Ranch after Pete French was killed. According to Brogan, Hill said to Hanley, an old friend, "I was building the railroad to come and see you."

The story of the last great outdoor railroad war in the United States, fought to a draw in the Deschutes Canyon of Central Oregon, causes a thoughtful person to wonder: If Hill and Harriman had been in their prime, full of beans and rarin' to go, would they have laid track side by side south from Bend, perhaps all the way to Mexico City?

James J. Hill driving the gold spike at Bend, 1911

THE BACKGROUND

It is not surprising that the last great railroad war was fought in Oregon. Railroads were late in coming to the state, suffered immense growing pains and generally have been less important to Oregon's growth than they were in other Western States.

Why? The answer probably lies in Oregon's rivers.

Steamboats solved most of the early transportation problems. The Willamette River and its tributaries made easy travel routes through the area of the first heavy settlement. The Columbia, on its long march to the sea, took care of another great strip of territory. Consequently early Oregonians were more immune to the railroad fever which infected most of the United States during the last half of the 19th century.

Two names stand out in early Oregon railroading — Henry Villard and Ben Holladay. Villard, the more important, laid 700 miles of track in Oregon, Holladay 240. Villard picked up the pieces of Holladay's railroading dreams, then, after a mighty effort, also went under.

Holladay was a hit-and-run operator with more than a trace of pirate's blood, shaky financial backing and a tremendous gift for making enemies. Villard was an intelligent, conservative man with a great aptitude for management and usually plenty of money. They were completely different types, yet both failed to build a railroad empire in stubborn Oregon...

In 1865, a California group calling itself the California and Oregon Railroad Company set out to build a line from Marysville, north of Sacramento, to Portland. The work was slow; only 90 miles of track had been built by 1870. Then the California and Oregon Railroad Company was swallowed up by the Central Pacific.

Oregonians suddenly got interested. More than a railroad was involved, because the federal government in those days, to encourage laying of track, gave large land grants to successful builders. The first Oregon group called itself Oregon Central Railroad Company. Soon the group split in two, but each kept the name and each started building south from Portland in 1868, one down the west side of the Willamette River, the other down the east side. Quickly the opposing sides came to be called East Siders and West Siders.

Henry Villard

The East Siders stumbled around in confusion until Ben Holladay bulled in from San Francisco to roar, "Let me in on this!"

The East Siders were delighted to oblige. Holladay had gained fame with his Overland Stage Lines but the wheels of the coaches were grinding to a halt. Railroads were about to take over land transportation and Holladay had been quick to read the future.

With Holladay providing the drive (and, some say, the bribe money) the government nodded toward the East Siders. If they could have 20 miles of line in operation by Christmas Day, 1869, the ripe land grant plum would fall into their laps.

Holladay, fighting floods and equipment shortages, won the race by little more than hours, sending the locomotive "J. B. Stephens," a baggage car and two coaches across the rails to a point about six miles south of Oregon City on December 23.

By 1871, Holladay had trains running between Portland and Eugene, and to Roseburg by the end of 1872.

Rails once carried most of Oregon's timber

Then Ben Holladay went broke...

Enter Henry Villard, off a boat from Germany. He had been sent to protect the interests of German financiers who had invested heavily in Oregon.

Villard went to work at cleaning up the debris left by Holladay. Little building was done during his first few years but in 1881, tracks were laid south of Roseburg. By 1884, the rails touched Ashland. In addition, Villard had become president of Northern Pacific and had brought this transcontinental line into Portland.

At which point Oregon railroading claimed another victim — Henry Villard went broke, his empire smashed by a national financial panic.

After three years, Edward H. Harriman and the Southern Pacific took over, thus setting the stage for the later Hill-Harriman battle in Deschutes Canyon. The Southern Pacific in 1887 provided Oregon's first rail link with California by ramming the rails through the massive Siskiyou Mountains. Stagecoaches had needed seven days for the trip between Portland and Sacramento; behind a steam locomotive, the trip required only 38 hours.

Much of the right-of-way of those early railroads still carries trains in Oregon, although the main line of the Southern Pacific now crosses the Cascades east of Eugene and bores into California through Klamath Falls.

The Deschutes Canyon passage over which Hill and Harriman fought so bitterly still is in use by trains. Some of this present line runs over the Hill right-of-way, some over Harriman's.

Portland marked Ben Holladay's short, stormy tenure in Oregon by naming a park and a street after him.

Henry Villard gave substantial amounts of money to the University of Oregon; Villard Hall, second building on the campus, is named for him.

Railroaders in Oregon who once fought each other have a new enemy — the giant trucks which now snort down all our highways. Perhaps it's just as well that the battlers of Deschutes Canyon didn't live long enough to tackle this opponent.

SUGGESTED READING

Adams, Kramer A.; LOGGING RAILROADS OF THE WEST; Superior; 1961.

Logging locomotives

CHAPTER TEN – Logging:
THE SKY AFIRE

August 14, 1933, dawned in western Oregon as just another hot and dry summer day. There had been many such days during the previous two months. Forests throughout the state shimmered under a cruel sun which drove all moisture out of the air and sucked the last juices of life from dead timber on the forest floor.

Loggers working northwest of Forest Grove in Washington County grumbled at the rising heat and looked forward to an afternoon of pinochle playing in the shade of the bunkhouse. At noon, all logging operations stopped when it became plain that during the afternoon ahead, a single spark might trigger a catastrophe.

All logging operations stopped, that is, except one...

At this camp in Gales Creek Canyon, a whistle blew at 1 p. m. to send the loggers back to work. A windfall cedar, bone-dry for years, lay in the path of a fir log being dragged to the landing. The fir and the cedar rubbed together, nothing more, but it was enough to bring into play a principle of physics well known to all Boy Scouts: fire by friction.

A wisp of smoke curled up from the logs.

Then came the terrible cry: "Fire!"

Within moments, Oregon's worst forest disaster was in the making. The Tillamook Burn was about to scorch its way into history.

Soon lookouts, staring from high in their isolated towers across one of the finest stands of timber in the world, spotted the smoke and reported it to Forest Grove headquarters.

Fire in the woods

One hundred men were sent to Gales Creek Canyon to aid the logging crew in confining the fire. At this moment, it was only a routine fight against a small blaze, the kind of exercise that fire-fighting crews experience hundreds of times during a normal summer in Oregon.

They worked with shovels and saws and picks through that afternoon building what is known as a "fire line," a cleared trail around the fire which would keep it from moving on the ground. But this fire refused to stay within the lines. The firefighters' worst enemy, wind, had entered the battle.

Soon after 6 p. m., a report came from several miles south of Gales Creek Canyon that a new blaze was burning south of the Wilson River road. The wind had struck its first hard blow.

The tempo of the battle increased. Trucks loaded with men from other logging camps were rushed to the scene. From Forest Grove came a crew of boys from the C. C. C. (Civilian Conservation Corps, something like the Job Corps of today).

The battle continued through the night. Miles of new fire line were built. Just as it appeared that the spread of flames might be halted, the fire "crowned," that is, leaped into the tops of centuries-old firs as tall as 11- or 12-story buildings. Whipped by wind, the flames raced through the treetops, laughing with crackling scorn at the puny fire lines far below, storming into many new areas where mighty trees stood defenseless before the white-hot attack.

Men came by the hundreds from Portland to join the fight. For almost five days the battle raged. Then, on Saturday night, August 19, the firefighters began to smell victory. The cruel wind had fallen off; Sunday might be a day of rest, after all.

But the wind had other plans...

On Sunday afternoon, it gathered its breath and blew the fire into the treetops again and sent the flames racing toward Reeher, where there were several more C. C. C. camps. The warning went ahead of the fire; the camps were evacuated in the nick of time.

There was no longer any doubt at Forest Grove headquarters about the nature of the enemy; this was a big one, a bad one, and many more days of horror were in store for northwestern Oregon.

Forest Grove quickly took on the look of an army camp just behind the front lines. Trucks rolled out of many points in Oregon

144

Smoke pall over the Tillamook Burn

and Washington and raced toward the Washington County town bearing men, equipment and supplies. The U. S. Army moved in to tackle the supply problem. Private lumber companies and state and federal forest agencies sent all available men.

The massive effort paid off. By August 24, the seemingly hopeless battle had taken a turn for the better. Forty thousand acres of prime timber had been burned but the wind was dying and the humidity rising. Hope crept into the hearts of weary, soot-blackened men on the fire lines.

It was a false hope. The enemy apparently had brought in reinforcements, too.

During the night of August 24-25, humidity tumbled freakishly until it stood at a horrifying 26 per cent at dawn, almost a record low for that hour. As if this weren't enough, an east wind, always warm and dry in August, swept into the fire area.

Lynn Cronemiller, state forester at the time, ordered everyone away from the west side of the blaze. He knew that the monster would now charge at full speed toward the sea.

The worst soon happened; the fire exploded, blew up, became a "firestorm" and lunged through the treetops at 60 or 70 miles an hour, lapping up everything in its path with a hot and hungry breath. A firestorm doesn't need natural wind to push it along; it creates its own wind through another simple principle of physics: warm air rises. Superheated air in the hottest parts of the blaze leaped toward the sky; cooler air around the fringes rushed in to fill the gaps. Result: high velocity wind.

(Anyone who lives in western Oregon feels the same effect on almost every summer day. As inland air warms and rises, cooler air off the ocean moves in to replace it. But cooling afternoon breezes are usually light and very welcome; multiply this effect by 20 and you have the winds of a firestorm.)

In northwestern Oregon on August 25, 1933, the firestorm took the shape of a towering curtain of flame 15 miles wide. Smoke rolled upward almost 10,000 feet high over the flames. Portlanders fifty miles away watched in awe as the massive white cloud appeared in the western sky.

A most graphic account of such a fire appeared in "Everybody's Magazine", December, 1910. Read and remember:

"The stillness of desolation rested above camps and towns where men by hundreds lived. There was no carrying power in the

146

air; sounds were muffled as if by a vacuum. Bewildered birds fluttered through the smoky chaos, panting, lost. Horses strained at their halters, looking upon their masters with questioning eyes, uncomforted by caresses, unassured by words. If a beast, by a terrified lunge, broke its restraining tether, it dashed away into the wilderness. Even dooryard fowls here and there deserted their coops, seeking a refuge at the margin of some stream. Dwellers in the woods and travelers on the dim trails saw forest creatures flying in one general direction, as if pursued by a force that struck a deeper terror than man. The fear of man, indeed, seemed lost in them. Scarcely would bear, mountain lions, or deer lift their heads at sight of a man or move out of his path to let him pass.

"A great tragedy was imminent in nature . . . there came at length a timid wind, sighing through the tree-walled canyons. It struck hot upon the forehead, it burned dry upon the lips, ruffling the smoke mantle for a moment, soon to die away . . . It freshened steadily, rolling away the smoke, showing the sun red as iron under the smith's hammer, far down near the edge of the world.

"That was all the warning the tempest of fire gave. It was as if it indulged the oft-voiced desire of dying men to look once more upon the sun. Out of the Northwest, over the mountains, it came. Bearing flaming brands . . . it came. Howling, roaring, the fires, but a few minutes before miles away, were upon the hamlets and camps, upon the lone cabins of settlers, leaping up the green mountain sides, streaming across canyons their long banners of obliterating flames . . .

"It swept uphill and downhill with unabated speed, although a fire in a mountain country usually rushes up hillsides much faster than it burns down. When the vanguard of the fire reached a canyon, it merely leaped across, no matter how wide the chasm. In one known instance it leaped a mile . . . The flames caught the resinous foliage and long streamers of . . . moss with the hissing roar of great skyrockets. In a breath, the proudest, oldest knights in this ancient guard of the mountains were stripped . . . their blackened trunks hurled to the ground by the tempest which drove the wild ocean of fire before it.

"Living man has not witnessed a more appalling sight. Days afterward, men who went through it were struck dumb in their struggle for words to measure its horrors. 'The world was afire,' they said, 'the earth, the air, everything.' Lightning flashed out of the great clouds of smoke; incandescent flames, burning like

147

carbon gas, sprang up, whistling their sharp notes above the roar of tempest and fire and the crash of falling trees, sprang up with nothing to feed on but air. In the superheated atmosphere it appeared that all nature had become outlawed . . . ''

The great cloud of 1933 hung over northwestern Oregon for two days. Lights were turned on in Forest Grove during the middle of the day as a kind of eerie half-night settled over the area. Hot embers and ashes drifted to the ground over hundreds of square miles. Evacuees poured out of the scorched earth, seeking any haven where the air was fit to breathe.

Even whole tops of trees were carried aloft by the rushing east winds and blown out to sea along with a vast amount of smaller debris, most of it still hot. All of it sizzled down into the ocean, then was washed back to shore on incoming tides. For many miles along the Oregon coast, the ashes of Oregon's worst forest fire were piled two feet deep in black, ugly heaps.

Finally, when it seemed that all of western Oregon's woodland might be ravished by flames, nature abruptly switched sides in the battle. A blanket of cool, moist fog slid in from the ocean, drove the fire out of the treetops to the ground and the worst was over. Suddenly fire lines were useful again; the monster was caged and beaten to death. It died slowly, though; pockets of fire still smoldered for months afterward.

Now began the sad job of measuring the damage. More than 311,000 acres had burned, much of it in Tillamook County in the last mad rush of the monster toward the sea. Throughout the area, Douglas fir which had grown unmolested for over 400 years stood stripped and charred; other mighty trees had been toppled by the firestorm and lay on the blackened earth defenseless before a new enemy — hordes of wood-eating insects.

The amount of prime timber burned was set at twelve and one-half billion board feet. By itself, that figure is just a figure. To appreciate the loss, one must realize that this number represents enough timber for all of the building that took place in the United States in 1932.

Work went ahead at full speed in the burn to cut and market all the timber which could be saved from the hungry billions of insects which would soon move in to finish the job of destruction.

It is an ill wind, they say, which blows no good. The terrible Tillamook fire of 1933 helped to awaken Oregonians — and all

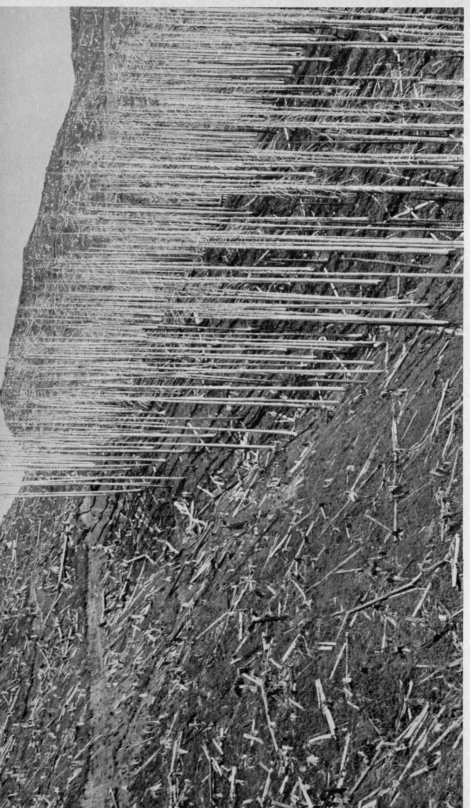

Snags left after the Tillamook fire

Americans — to the need for protecting forests against the carelessness of human beings. When part of the area burned over in 1933 suffered again in a 1939 blaze and then still again in 1945, the public outcry resulted in legislative action. State money for reforestation became available in 1949; work started immediately.

By 1965, the work had been largely finished. That is, most of the burn area had been re-planted, hundreds of miles of roads had been built and snags had been cleared from long, wide corridors to help prevent another disastrous fire. The remainder of the work, the growing of giant Douglas fir to match those which burned, must be left to nature in the centuries ahead.

Effects of the fire are still painfully plain to anyone who drives between Forest Grove and the coast, even though young trees and other vegetation are creeping back over the once-black slopes.

But it is not enough to plant trees. Once growing, they must be protected from natural enemies, the most dangerous of which is man himself. The work of protection has been helped immensely by the Keep Oregon Green Association, which has enrolled thou-

School Conservation tour in Benton County

Replanting the Tillamook Burn

sands of Oregon boys and girls, ages 8-16, in the Oregon Green Guard. Annual conservation tours take Oregon sixth graders into the woods for on-the-spot instruction in forest lore. During 1964, such tours were held in 30 of Oregon's 36 counties, with almost 20,000 school children taking part.

Some of the seedlings which are growing now in the Tillamook Burn were planted by Oregon schoolchildren. If those seedlings are to reach the towering heights of the trees which were carelessly destroyed in 1933, many more generations of young Oregonians will have to help. No one living now can hope to see another forest in northwestern Oregon like the one which burned in 1933. A tree grows in its own good time, ignoring the calendars of man.

But modern Oregonians can leave a priceless heritage to the generations to come. In a land increasingly blighted by the crowding together of people, by the pollution of the air and water, by the nerve-shattering noise of modern life, our forests may be more important to our peace of mind than they ever were, even if not one more house is built from their timber.

The cool and sun-dappled forest offers quiet, soaring beauty in a society where this quality has become rare and precious. Oregon today has more of this treasure than any other place in the world.

But like any treasure, it must be guarded. A forest is an accident of nature. Under certain conditions of soil and climate, like those we have in Oregon, great trees will grow from a handful of seeds.

An accident of nature creates them; an accident of man can wipe them out.

THE BACKGROUND

Fire, now the major enemy of Oregon forests, once was used as a tool by farmers in clearing Oregon land for the plow. Unhappily, these man-set fires often escaped into the foothills and highlands. It is estimated that in the hundred years of Oregon settlement before 1911, major fires burned over four million acres and destroyed 160 billion board feet of timber. That fantastic figure represents as much lumber as was produced in Oregon from 1900 through 1948!

The sky-blotting smoke palls which are unusual now once were ordinary. A Newport newspaper of 1853 reported that the coastal steamer "Pioneer" was unable to navigate through the

152

Trees grow again in the Tillamook Burn

smoke. A Captain Turnbull of the riverboat "Fannie Troup" suggested in 1868 that lighthouses might be necessary along the Willamette to enable steamers to find their way along the stream through the incessant smoke. A newspaper headline as late as 1902 shouted: "Smoke Stops Shipping — Thick Bank Prevents Vessels Reaching Columbia River."

There is reason to believe that Oregon has entered a bright new era of forest protection; there is reason to hope that the state will never again see another disaster in the woods as great as the Tillamook Burn. Wind, which fanned the Tillamook flames, may have proved that we have come a long way since 1933.

On Columbus Day, 1962, an historic storm sneaked into southern Oregon off the Pacific Ocean, then whined and moaned over the western part of the state, gathering strength as it moved northward. Winds reached a velocity of more than 100 miles an hour at Portland.

As the tempest passed through the forests, great swaths of timber were smashed to the ground. Within a few hours, 9.6 billion board feet of Oregon trees were snapped off and uprooted, more than two-thirds the amount destroyed in the Tillamook Burn.

Immediately Keep Oregon Green and other forest protection agencies stepped up their work. Newspapers around the state told the citizens of Oregon, then told them again and again, that the fire danger during the summer of 1963 would be the greatest in history because the forest floor in many parts of western Oregon was covered with blowdown timber. As the dry season approached, firefighting crews were strengthened and put on the alert.

Oregon citizens responded. During the fire season of 1963, with great sections of woodland choked with fuel awaiting a careless spark, only 11,848 acres burned. Almost as much had burned in 1962, during the summer before the great storm.

The work of salvaging the blowdown timber went ahead at full speed. Even so, a great amount of it remained when the fire season of 1964 approached. Again the public was given a special warning. Again the effort paid off. During the summer of 1964 only 7721 acres burned, less than in any year since 1953.

The crisis years had passed without a terrible tragedy. Oregon citizens had reason to be proud of their forest agencies, public and private, and the agencies had as much reason to be

Early log hauling by cable

proud of Oregonians, both young and old. (Oregonians have always been more woods-wise than persons living in other parts of the country. Around the nation, 90 per cent of all forest fires are man-caused; in Oregon, only 50 per cent.)

New methods of conservation and firefighting no doubt helped. Forestry experts have taken to the air in their battle against the enemies of the trees. Re-seeding from airplanes was tried in the Tillamook Burn with considerable success. Aerial spraying against insect enemies also has proved effective.

Airplanes now have taken over a share of the work of fire prevention and firefighting. The lonely lookout on his isolated tower may be on the way out; airplanes and helicopters may be able to do a better job at lower cost. Large airplanes, frequently converted World War II bombers, are used widely for the dropping of chemicals which retard and suppress fire in the woods. (The authors vividly remember watching a B-17, the famous "Flying Fortress" of World War II, wing in from its base at Medford to drop a great purple cloud of chemical over a fire in Josephine County in 1962. This is a sight not easily forgotten.)

Most glamorous of the airborne firefighters, though, are the "smokejumpers," trained parachutists who leap into the trees near a fire with tools and extinguishers, then go to work stifling a blaze far sooner than was formerly possible. The smokejumper's job is to keep small fires small; if smokejumpers had been available in 1933, there might have been no Tillamook Burn. Training centers for these firefighters of the sky are maintained near Cave Junction in Josephine County and near Redmond in Deschutes County.

* * * * *

How important is the timber industry to Oregon?

No less important than life and breath to Oregonians.

Statistics tell a plain story: Nearly one-fourth of the softwood lumber, over half of the plywood and more than one-fourth of the hardboard produced in the United States come from Oregon.

The stand of salable timber in Oregon is 500.3 billion board feet. (Converted to lumber, this amount of forest would be enough to rebuild completely every home in the United States, with enough left over for schools and hospitals.)

Forest industry employment provides 54 per cent of manufacturing payrolls in Oregon.

The old way in the woods

Since 1938 Oregon has led the United States in timber production.

The plywood industry is rated the second fastest growing industry in the nation; only the plastics industry exceeds it. Oregon took the lead in the plywood field in 1936 and still holds it. Plywood was invented in Oregon; the first sheets were made at a box and barrel factory in the St. Johns district of Portland. (Unhappily, one of those first sheets burned in 1964 when fire destroyed the huge log structure called the Forestry Building in Portland, which had been a famous forest museum.)

* * * * *

Oregon's timber area is divided neatly into two parts: the Douglas fir region west of the Cascade Mountains and the ponderosa pine region east of the mountains. Other kinds of trees are cut in both areas but fir and pine are the most important. (Oregon's most famous tree species, the Douglas fir, was named after David Douglas, a pioneer botanist.)

Lane County and Douglas County top the state in timber production. Lane County grabbed the lead in log production from Clatsop County in 1941, then lost out to Douglas County in 1949. In the early 1960's, however, Lane again took over the lead.

In eastern Oregon's pine region, Grant County is the leader, followed by Klamath, Lake, Union and Umatilla counties.

Timber harvesting methods, like conservation and firefighting methods, have changed with the times. In the early days, much timber was dragged out of the woods behind ox teams, then floated down the rivers to market. Then a network of logging railroads took over the job. Now most of this work is done by the giant trucks which are a familiar sight on Oregon's highways. (And a familiar cause of stark terror for out-of-state tourists who meet one of these monsters bellowing down a winding mountain road.)

Yet, with all the changes, loggers continued to wish for a mythical "skyhook" from which they could string the cables and pulleys needed to drag logs out of the woods and down to the loading point.

In 1964, the myth became reality. Goodyear Aerospace designed and built a huge triangular balloon, filled it with helium and tried it out in Oregon forests.

Log loading, 1905

It worked. All the rigging needed to move logs could be attached to this point in the sky 500 feet above the earth. The balloon could be raised or lowered as needed simply by paying out or taking in its tether. With the balloon method, it appeared that much less building of expensive roads would be necessary for the logging of high, remote stands of timber.

"Vee-Ballons," as Goodyear calls them, were still in the experimental stage in 1965. Early promise, however, indicates that we might live to see the day when an Oregon logging operation will be marked not by its ox teams or donkey engine but by its gas bag floating high above the forest.

The skyhook-dreamers, the generations of mighty men who worked in the Oregon woods down the years, surely would have dropped their axes in amazement.

SUGGESTED READING

Johnson, Jalmar; BUILDERS OF THE NORTHWEST; Dodd, Mead; 1963.

Stoutenburg, Adrien, and Baker, Laura Nelson; WILD TREASURE: THE STORY OF DAVID DOUGLAS; Scribner's; 1958.

Modern logging by **Vee-Balloon**

CHAPTER ELEVEN – Shipping:
WINDOW ON THE WORLD

It can be said with some justification that Oregon floated into history.

Water, both salt and fresh, provided highways for explorers and food to sustain them. Water, falling over the Willamette Valley at a rate of 55-60 inches each year, produced the lush, year-around carpet of greenery which attracted settlers. Water and snow, drenching the highlands, fed the conifer seedlings which were to become the giants of the forest and the foundation of a great industry. Water, foaming through great dams, generates the electric power which keeps Oregon humming.

It is hardly surprising, then, that the national image of Oregon is a wet one. The typical Oregon student, trudging toward school during December in Tillamook or Salem or Eugene with water soaking his shoes and dripping from the end of his nose, wouldn't argue with that national image. To that student, Oregon seems like the wettest place in the world. To tell that student that without water, Oregon wouldn't amount to much, would only invite a sneer and a snarl. To tell that same student that Californians and Arizonans are working mightily to take some of that water away from us would only bring the comment: "Terrific! Let me know if they need any help!"

But hold on a minute . . .

Without water, there would be no Columbia and Willamette rivers; without water, there would be few products to ship along those rivers; without the rivers and the products, there would be no Port of Portland; with no port, the largest city in Oregon might today be a sleepy little hamlet where the natives tended their roses by day and rested in their rocking chairs by night.

Sailing vessel at Portland wharf

Without the Columbia River running along its northern border, Oregon's past would have been less glorious, its future much less bright. The great length, enormous flow and rapid fall of the Columbia makes it one of the world's greatest sources of water power. In this respect, the Columbia outranks the Mississippi River and the Volga in Russia; in its value to man, it towers over the Ganges River of India, the Euphrates of Iraq, the Yangtze of China, the Yukon of Alaska and the Amazon of South America. A full one-third of the water power potential of continental United States is in the basin of the Columbia River. Furthermore, the Columbia gives inland Portland its only deepwater shipping lane to the sea.

The "port" in "Portland" is no accident. From the earliest days of settlement on the Tualatin Plains, farmers needed a shipping point for their products. During the last half of the 19th century, sailing ships crossed the dangerous bar at Astoria, entered the Columbia, set their sails against the surging current of the second largest river system in America, veered to starboard at the mouth of the Willamette, then docked in Portland to unload cargoes in a growing country and take on food and lumber for eager customers around the world.

It was a good beginning. It is hardly surprising that modern Portland is split down its middle by 17 miles of harbor facilities. Once every five hours, on the average, a ship enters the harbor. More than eight per cent of Portland's jobs result directly or indirectly from harbor activity.

A deepwater harbor is like the small end of a funnel; it collects what is poured into the big end. Port of Portland serves an inland area as large as all of New England. Barges churn up the Columbia and in combination with trucks, make the funnel 250 miles long. (Even much longer if you count shipments from other parts of the country.)

Barley and wheat grown in the inland empires of Oregon, Washington and Idaho (and some from as far away as the Midwest) are poured into the big end of the funnel in vast quantities, enough to make Portland the Pacific Coast's leading grain port. Terminal No. 4 in the Portland harbor, at the foot of N. Lombard Street, boasts the largest grain elevator on tidewater west of the Mississippi River. From this elevator, ships can be loaded at the rate of 1200 tons per hour. (Perhaps the figure is meaningless to anyone but the farm boy who has shovelled a hundred bushels of

Portland waterfront in 1905

grain under a hot sun; 1200 tons represents more than 31,000 bushels. Moral: If you have grain to ship these days, let Port of Portland shovel it for you.)

It wasn't always like this. The first salt water commerce in the Portland area didn't come to Portland at all for a very good reason: There wasn't any Portland at the time. Small sailing ships started up the Columbia during the first half of the last century to unload supplies at Dr. McLoughlin's Fort Vancouver and to load a cargo of furs for the return trip around Cape Horn to the Atlantic ports. When Portland became a going concern about 1845, some of the ships turned into the Willamette a few miles north west of present Vancouver, threaded their way through the dangerous passage along Swan Island (which was then really an island; now, because of land filling, it's a peninsula) and nudged the landing to take on the growing quantities of farm produce from the Willamette Valley and lumber from the small sawmills which were setting up in the wooded hills around the little frontier community.

It was not as easy as it sounds for those early sailing ship captains. Portland is unique among major Pacific Coast ports in that it is 110 miles inland; Los Angeles and San Francisco offer sheltered harbors within hailing distance of the open ocean; Seattle is on Puget Sound, which is really just a huge arm of the sea.

One hundred and ten miles of river travel may not sound like much of a chore for a ship designed to survive the dangers of open ocean but rivers, particularly ones as long and mighty as the Columbia, have sneaky little tricks of their own. They have a bad habit of picking up tons of sand and depositing it in unlikely places. A ship well-stuck on a sand bar might as well be tied to a wharf. Many a ship captain has studied a navigation chart showing an open channel in the Columbia and steered a careful course only to fall on his face as his craft ground to a painful halt on a sand bar that wasn't there when his chart was printed.

There is a record of a certain Captain Menes of the French bark "Morning Star" who, when his ship went aground on a sand bar at the mouth of the Columbia, immediately stepped to the rail and threw all his charts overboard.

Captain Menes was by no means the only skipper who ever lost his patience and his ship at the mouth of the Columbia River. It was not long after Captain Robert Gray's discovery of the

Columbia in 1792 that the entrance into the Northwest's greatest river developed a worldwide reputation as one of the most dangerous traps into which a ship could be sailed. The area soon became a graveyard for ships; hulks of the foolish or unlucky ones still mark the cemetery. (The spot where the "Peter Iredale" went aground on Clatsop Beach in 1906 is now a state park.)

Sand, billions of fine grains of it carried by the strong-flowing river, formed underwater ridges when the fresh water struck the incoming tides of the salt ocean. Sometimes sand piled in great soft heaps so high that it jutted above the water to form an island at low tide, then hid beneath the surface when the tide flowed in and waited for a victim.

There have been many victims. During the years between 1850 and 1950, there were 150 major shipwrecks in the area around the mouth of the Columbia.

The shifting sand had a strong ally in the storms which frequently batter the northern Oregon coast. With a storm blowing, wise captains learned to anchor off the mouth in deep water. Even in fair weather, danger lurked. Navigation charts couldn't be printed fast enough to warn of the shifting sands. Pilots sent out from Astoria to guide incoming ships through the maze of sandbars sometimes made mistakes, with ships and men paying the price. Once hung up on a bar, a ship was at the mercy of a new storm. Wind and waves often made short work of destroying their helpless prey.

Jetties were constructed on both sides of the river mouth to control the sand buildup and keep a channel open. Dredging helped, too. Navigational aids such as lighthouses and buoys were installed to mark the safe path. World War II brought the wide use of radar on ships. With each step, the mouth of the Columbia became a little less terrifying. But man is still not the complete master of a mighty river and a wild ocean; he may never be. Ships still go aground; lives are still lost in the surging sea; it is not likely that the captain of a ship will ever suffer from boredom while entering the salt water gate to the Port of Portland.

As Portland and Oregon grew during the 1880's, it became plain that something would have to be done about those pesky, sand-logged rivers if new and larger ships were to be accommodated. Even the relatively small ships operating out of San Francisco had taken to docking at St. Helens, 30 miles from Portland, to avoid the dangers of the plugged-up upper Columbia and Willam-

Mouth of the

bia at Astoria

ette. Any vessel drawing over 17 feet of water (that is, sinking deeper than that into the water) did not stand much chance of reaching Portland.

Unless something was done to provide a deeper, safer channel, Portland was finished as a saltwater port. In 1891, the Port of Portland, a municipal taxing district, was formed to deal with the problem.

First, dikes were built to encourage the rivers to drop their loads of sand somewhere else. They did not work very well. Something else was needed; dredging was turned to.

River dredging is essentially a simple process. Sand is picked up from the shipping channel and dumped somewhere else. If you want to, you can make new land by dumping the sand where it will be useful. (This is how Swan Island became a peninsula instead of an island.)

First, the Port of Portland took over an old "chain-and-bucket" dredge which had been used to cut through the sand at the head of Swan Island. It wasn't nearly good enough and was soon junked.

A chain-and-bucket dredge was nothing more than a mechanized shovel; something stronger and faster was needed. It was provided in 1898 when the first hydraulic suction dredge went into operation. Naturally enough, it bore the name "Portland."

What the "Portland" did was suck the sand into a 20-inch pipe, then spew it out through several hundred additional feet of pipe into a place where it wouldn't block the channel. Think of a huge floating vacuum cleaner and you have the "Portland." The "Portland" worked in the rivers until 1922, when an ungrateful ship collided with it and sank it.

No matter; 30-inch dredges were at work. Four of these have been provided by the Port of Portland, worked to death, then disposed of . . . all but one, the "Clackamas," which sucked at the rivers furiously for 39 years, then was retired with honors in 1964. In 1965, the new dredge "Oregon" was delivered, which will dig deeper and pump much farther than the "Clackamas" ever could.

Once a suction dredge went into operation, the days of a 17-foot channel were over. Work began in 1913 on a plan to dredge and maintain a 30-foot channel. It was about this time that the

170

Modern Portland harbor

federal government began to take an active interest in development of the ship channel which serves Portland harbor. Since 1913, the U. S. Army Engineers, supplying money, equipment and personnel, have given the Port of Portland a big boost in its work on the waterways which are the veins and arteries of Oregon.

In 1930, a 35-foot channel project got underway. In January, 1964, work began on a channel 40 feet deep and 600 feet wide throughout the 110 miles of sand-loaded river which separates Portland from the sea. Plans call for completion in 1968.

It is safe to say that Portland's future as an ocean port, which hung by a small hawser in 1891, is now secure. As fast as the Columbia and Willamette Rivers pump sand into the channel, giant dredges will pump it out.

This is important for reasons which have nothing to do with the business of money-making. A fair share of Portland's charm as a city results from its harbor activity. There will always be something especially romantic, even in a day of space travel, in the sight of a proud ship from a far distant land sliding along the Columbia and Willamette rivers to a berth in the land called Oregon. Name America's most interesting cities and in most cases, you find yourself naming saltwater ports — New York, Philadelphia, New Orleans, San Diego, Los Angeles, San Francisco, Seattle . . . and Portland.

Exotic products from exotic lands pour into Portland each day. What do we need from other countries? Well, let's start with spices, flavors, cocoa, dates, sesame seeds and coconut. Our bakeries need them all. Then there's rattan, nut meats and horseradish (yes, horseradish). Other food processors need these. Manufacturers of paper products import tapioca starch. Drapery manufacturers must have bamboo and linen. The lumber industry needs Swedish steel. Refrigeration equipment demands imported cork. Belgian glass is used in aluminum doors and windows. The chemical industry uses manganese, carnauba wax (this will leave a shine on your hot rod like nothing else), bauxite and coconut oil.

But foreign trade over the oceans is by no means a one-way street. If we want to sell in other countries, we must buy in other countries. Anyone who is worried about foreign goods flooding the United States should take a look at the Port of Portland figures for 1970: nearly two and one-half tons shipped to foreign ports for each ton brought in.

172

Portland waterfront in 1900

Portland's best customer, by far, is Japan. In 1970, Portland sent more than five tons of goods to Japan for each ton received in return. America is not likely to be flooded with Japanese transistor radios; it is more likely that we will flood Japan with our grain and timber.

All sorts of strange things pass across the Port of Portland wharves. Onions, for instance. Exactly 3506 tons of these were shipped from Portland in 1970. You may believe it or not, but official statistics show that Portland also shipped 7713 tons of old newspapers and waste in 1970. To say nothing of 356 tons of dried prunes...

Much less frivolous, though, is the major Portland export: wheat to feed a hungry world. Two and one-half million tons of this food were shipped in 1970 from Portland and more than three million tons from other Columbia River ports.

Shipbuilding doesn't hold the important place in the Portland area that it occupied during World War I and World War II, although many smaller craft are still being built. During World War I, shipyards lined the river from Portland's central district to St. Johns and the work went on day and night. Most of the ships were built of wood from Oregon forests.

When World War II renewed the need for a great shipbuilding effort, the Portland area again was called upon, even though these ships were to be made of iron and steel. An industrialist named Henry Kaiser ran a spectacular show in his shipbuilding yards at Swan Island, St. Johns and at Vancouver across the Columbia. Faced with a labor shortage, Kaiser simply hauled trainloads of workers in from the East. When housing was needed for these thousands of men, Kaiser built two cities — Vanport City north of Portland and McLoughlin Heights near Vancouver. (At its peak, Vanport was the second largest city in Oregon.) During those years, Portland became a shipbuilding town; ships produced in Oregon waters played an important part in winning the war.

Oregon still offers a startling reminder of those wartime years in the U. S. Navy's "mothball fleet" moored near Astoria. At war's end, hundreds of ships were tied up, gunwale to gunwale, in a sheltered bay at Tongue Point to be preserved for possible future use. Their gun turrets were coated with plastic and other measures were taken to keep the salt air from eating away the metal.

It is fitting that these ships should be stored at Astoria, which was Oregon's first ocean port and remains an important one. Astoria's commercial fishing fleet is the largest in the state. (Astoria also is proud of 125-foot Astor Column, built in 1926. Anyone willing to climb its circular staircase can enjoy one of the most awesome views in Oregon — the mighty Columbia as it meets the ocean head-on.)

Other important coastal ports include Newport, which is the world's second largest lumber shipping port, and Coos Bay.

While the Port of Portland has shown remarkable growth in waterborne commerce, it hasn't neglected the air, either. Portland's first airport was developed by the Port on Swan Island. Charles Lindbergh, first pilot to cross the Atlantic, dedicated the field in 1927 after flying to Portland in the "Spirit of St. Louis."

Portland air traffic soon outgrew Swan Island and was moved to its present site in east Portland in 1940. The Port of Portland continues to operate what has become in the jet age one of the nation's fastest-growing airports, Portland International. Approximately two and one-half million passengers hurried through its sprawling terminal in 1970.

Largest ship drydocked at Swan Island

Swan Island, where Henry Kaiser built ships during World War II, now boasts one of the best drydock facilities on the Pacific Coast. (Just to keep its head in the clouds, the Port also operates a helicopter base on the island.) An ocean port of substantial size needs ship repair facilities. Portland had none until 1901, when the first was built in the St. Johns district. Dry Dock No. 3 at Swan Island is rated the third largest on the Pacific Coast.

One of the most startling sights of Portland harbor, though, is what seems to be a ghost out of the past — a sternwheel steamboat. Named "Portland," this craft is not nearly so ancient as it looks. It was built in 1947. Owned by the Port authority, the big steamer is leased to a private tugboat company to use when a really big ship needs to be pushed around in Portland harbor. The "Portland," 219 feet long, is powered by two 900-horsepower steam engines.

Boats much like this one churned up and down the Columbia and Willamette rivers during the heyday of the river traffic. A view of the "Portland," with smoke streaming from its funnel

Portland International Airport

Sternwheeler "Portland" works in Portland harbor

and the water foaming behind its huge paddlewheel, is enough to gladden the heart of anyone interested in the most romantic era of American river transportation.

During 1970, 1406 ships arrived in Portland harbor. Of these, 179 were American, the remainder foreign. Of the foreign ships, Norway and Japan sent the most.

Oregon (and particularly Portland) is often accused of being stodgy, of looking inward too much while a fast-moving world passes it by. There may be some truth in this criticism.

But there is no denying that it has the Port of Portland, its window on the world.

THE BACKGROUND

Two rivers, the Columbia and Willamette, carried a mighty load in early Oregon transportation. One man above all others made those rivers work for Oregon.

The man was Captain John C. Ainsworth.

Rivers were the arteries which carried life blood through developing Oregon and Captain Ainsworth was the pumping heart.

He had been a steamboat captain on the Mississippi. He came west and took over command of the "Lot Whitcomb," first steamboat built on the Willamette. From then until 1879, when he sold his Oregon Steam Navigation Company to railroader Henry Villard, J. C. Ainsworth furnished most of the excitement in river transportation in Oregon.

Steamboating was a wild, swashbuckling, intensely competitive business in Oregon, just as it was along the Mississippi. The formula, in a transportation-hungry land, was simple: Build a big, fast boat with somebody else's money, put it into service, then pay for it quickly out of profits. Often a steamer would earn $3000 to $5000 profit on a single trip. The record was set in 1862 when a single boat, on just one trip on the Columbia, made $10,000. Steamboating was a speedy road to fame and fortune for a wise, bold man; a short path to bankruptcy for the losers of the battles which raged up and down American rivers.

In Oregon, Ainsworth was the winner. The "Lot Whitcomb" served nobly under its bewhiskered captain, then gave way to the "Jennie Clark". In turn, "Jennie Clark" was replaced by "Carrie Ladd". But competition chewed at Ainsworth's profits. In an attempt to regulate prices, he organized the Union Trans-

The steamboat "Lot Whitcomb"

portation System. This helped, but it had one great weakness; Union Transportation had no control over the owners of the portages which linked the three major sections of the Columbia.

In 1860, Ainsworth organized the Oregon Steam Navigation Company, which took the portage owners under its wing. Then luck took a hand. A gold rush in Idaho triggered profitable river traffic along the Columbia. O. S. N. commanded the river and J. C. Ainsworth commanded O. S. N.

Success bred success. Inland Oregon and Washington were settled by farmers. Great quantities of wheat poured into the holds of O. S. N. steamers and enough of those boats arrived in Portland to make the growing city one of the most important grain ports in the world.

The coming of railroads to Oregon cut heavily into the steamboat traffic. After selling O. S. N. to Villard, J. C. Ainsworth went to Oakland, California, and died there in 1893.

Tugs and barges and log rafts still churn up and down the Columbia and Willamette but much of the glamor and excitement is gone. Once, in the heyday of Ainsworth, huge and graceful steamboats stormed along the rushing waters, paused here and there along the banks to take on fuel for hungry fireboxes and to discharge passengers and cargo, then resumed their foaming path into one of the most colorful chapters of Oregon history.

In the old days, the hoarse wail of a steamboat whistle was a comforting sound in the damp darkness of an Oregon winter night. But those days are gone, just as Captain Ainsworth is gone. Romantic Oregonians are the losers, because there are no sights and sounds in the Oregon of today as exciting as the glorious commotion once created by an Ainsworth steamboat as it charged down the Columbia toward Astoria with pitch-pine smoke spewing from its funnel, with a frothy river waving a banner of defiance behind it.

SUGGESTED READING

Gibbs, James A., Jr.; PACIFIC GRAVEYARD; Binfords & Mort; 1950.

Johnson, Jalmar; BUILDERS OF THE NORTHWEST; Dodd, Mead; 1963.

Night work at Swan Island drydock

Willamette Valley and Mt. Hood

CHAPTER TWELVE – Land, Sea and Air

A modern boy or girl living in Oregon's Willamette Valley, staring up at an endlessly dripping winter sky or watching a flooding river lap at his front porch, has good reason to moan about his wet fate.

Another boy or girl in eastern Oregon, leaning into a dry desert windstorm, is moved to join the chorus of complaint.

Yet, if we can take a long, long view, all Oregonians, east and west, must admit that we never had it so good.

Believe it or not, Oregon was once an ocean.

Believe it or not, the Willamette Valley was not only once a salt ocean but later in its watery career became a fresh water lake.

Believe it or not, crocodiles and camels and elephants once lived in and around swamps in that eastern Oregon area where the dust now blows.

This, of course, was not yesterday. It was, in fact, almost 200 million years ago. (To understand fully how long ago that was, one must think of the length of the last day of the school year, then multiply that length by 100.)

We are not talking now about history; we are talking about what came before recorded history. "Prehistoric," in other words. We can't be absolutely sure that these conditions existed millions of years ago but wise persons wearing impressive titles like "geologist," "anthropologist" and "archaeologist" have been studying the area for many years and then making a lot of educated guesses.

What is now Oregon in history, these educated guesses tell

us, was a couple of huge islands in pre-history. There were no Cascade or Coast Ranges. Water-laden clouds which now dump billions of gallons of water on western Oregon each winter swept inland, then unloaded. Result: lakes, swamps, marshes and even oceans.

Then the land began to rise. Volcanic explosions took place; lava flowed into the great waters and land was formed. The two islands were connected. As volcanic explosions occurred and as the earth's crust shifted, broke and thrust rocky fingers upward, mountains were formed.

As soon as there were mountains, Oregon as we know it today began to take shape. Now the ocean storms blowing eastward were forced to rise when they struck the rocky barriers. In rising, the clouds cooled and lost their grip on their load of water. (Warm air can hold much more water than cold.) The water was dumped on the west side of the mountains. Eastern Oregon began to dry up.

The ocean we now call Pacific was pushed backward to its present shoreline by the Coast Range. When the great river we call Columbia was blocked by volcanic eruptions, its fresh water poured into the Willamette Valley, forming a lake. Eventually, as stream beds were cut through the Coast Range, this lake drained away, leaving in its wake some of the country's most fertile farm land. It also left a land that has fascinated archaeologists, geologists, paleontologists and anthropologists for many years.

So far as we know, most of these millions of years passed without a human being around to keep a diary. During this period, Oregon was strictly for the birds, animals and fishes. Man, as far as the prehistoric evidence showed, did not exist.

Then, in 1938, Dr. L. S. Cressman, an anthropologist from the University of Oregon, discovered a pair of sandals in a Lake County cave ...

The sandals were exposed to a radio-carbon test. (By using this method, students of pre-history have been able to pinpoint the age of materials much more closely than they ever could before.)

The radio-carbon test on the sandals found in Fort Rock Cave indicated that a being called human lived in Oregon 9000 years ago. Measured against the millions of years we've been dealing with, this is a mere tick of a clock.

The Fort Rock anthropologists found other traces of human life: baskets, knives, arrowheads and stones which apparently

Fort Rock

were used to weigh down fishnets.

What did the Fort Rock man look like? We can only guess. No skeletons have been found. Anthropologists and archaeologists may yet come up with an answer.

Other areas of Oregon have provided rich finds. The John Day fossil beds in Grant County have attracted miners of pre-historic lore since Thomas Condon, Oregon's pioneer geologist, first explored the area in 1865. (Fossils, incidentally, are traces of plant or animal life; even a footprint qualifies; a preserved bone is considered a rich find.)

Condon's later discoveries centered around Fossil Lake, in Lake County. The area was to become known as The Equus (horse) Beds of Oregon. Evidence was found of several types of horses which once roamed the country, along with elephants, camels and other mammals. The discovery attracted fossil hunters from all over the United States.

Perhaps the most interesting convulsion of the Oregon earth was that which produced Crater Lake, now a national park in Klamath County. Mount Mazama took a notion to blow its top, volcanically speaking, about 6600 years ago. (Those very early Oregonians living at Fort Rock not so far away must have thought the world was coming to an end when they saw the fire and were pelted with hot lava. The Jacksonville Museum has four large paintings which re-create this fantastic eruption.)

The top of the mountain fell back into the crater created by the explosion. Rainfall over thousands of years created a fantastic deep blue lake. Result: a rocky wonderland that is southern Oregon's prime tourist attraction.

The geologic story is plain: Oregon was born in water and lives by water. And yet the national image of Oregon as "that place where it rains all the time" is something of a lie ...

Actually, there is no single "Oregon climate." There are at least five Oregon climates. Most students of climate and weather lump western Oregon into one category and eastern Oregon into another. But both Astoria and Ashland are in western Oregon. Astoria has an average 78 inches of rainfall per year; Ashland has 20. The "summer" of northwestern Oregon may occur between July 15 and August 1; southwestern Oregon, on the other hand, almost always has 3-4 months of some of the hottest, driest weather one can find in the northern half of the country between

Columbia River at Crown Point

Mt. Hood from the southeast

May and September. In July, when Astoria may have 70 per cent humidity, a southern Oregon afternoon crackles with 27 per cent humidity and forest fire warnings.

Such differences also exist east of the Cascades. The cool, almost brisk summer of the high Wallowa Lake country hardly compares with the bristling heat of Klamath Falls or Bend.

The ocean and mountains create Oregon's climates. Eastern Oregon falls under what is known as a "rain shadow;" the clouds off the ocean, tapped by the Cascade Mountains, spill their water before they reach the eastern deserts. Marine storms, sweeping in during the winter from the Gulf of Alaska, and pushed inland by the prevailing winds out of the west, dump their loads in western Oregon. What moisture remains in the rising clouds after they clear the Cascades falls as snow on the sweeping eastern Oregon plateaus.

The wettest areas in Oregon are along the coast. To compensate, the areas of most even temperature, winter and summer, are also along the coast. During the occasional storm-free periods during the winter, when the inland valleys often fill with cold fog, coastal afternoons may be sun-bright and warm. As an added compensation for coastal residents, flowers bloom along the ocean shore in lush colors which put to shame the inland blooms.

While eastern Oregonians might covet the rains which wash over the west, they wouldn't trade for them the dry, brisk, sunlit days which highlight a winter east of the Cascades. While eastern Oregon eyes feast on Mt. Hood, Three Sisters and Broken Top, Willamette Valley residents snarl at fog and overcast.

Southern Oregonians may have the best of both worlds. Thirty inches of rainfall soak the lovely forested mountains in Josephine and Jackson Counties during a typical winter but summer always comes, hot and dry.

In eastern Oregon, only about 100 days in a year are free of frost; in western Oregon, the frost-free days are doubled. The single true word about Oregon climate is not "rain;" the single true word is "variety." Whatever climate one wants, Oregon offers it, from wet coast to dry desert . . . but one must know where to look. And wherever one looks, one must be ready to appreciate.

Oregon remains one of America's undiscovered wonderlands. California plunges ahead through smog and taxes toward a position as the most populated of all these United States. Washington tries, with some success, to follow.

Oregon, with a large chunk of this country's land area, still has only a small part of its population. Lapped by 400 miles of ocean, inspired by towering mountains, nourished by immense natural resources, Oregon must inevitably absorb its share of our country's exploding population. The day must come when the mountain trails and the ocean beaches, the looming forests and the far reach of desert will be quiet and empty no longer.

But if young Oregonians of today know and appreciate the goodness of their broad and beautiful land, it needn't all be lost; those old ones who saw Oregon as America's last frontier needn't be betrayed.

SUGGESTED READING

Fish, Ron, and Spring, Bob and Ira; THIS IS OREGON; Superior; 1957.

Glassley, Ray Hoard; VISIT THE PACIFIC NORTHWEST; Binfords & Mort; 1948.

Montgomery, Richard G.; YOUNG NORTHWEST; Random; 1941.

OREGON 1965-1966 BLUE BOOK; Secretary of State; 1965.

Parrish, Philip H.; HISTORIC OREGON; Macmillan; 1949.

Zim, Herbert S., and Dodge, Natt N.; THE PACIFIC NORTHWEST: Golden Press; 1959.

Grotto Cove at Crater Lake

OREGON FACTS AND FIGURES

Total area: 96,981 square miles (10th largest in U. S.)

Population: 2,091,385 (31st in U. S., 1970 census)

State capital: Salem

Counties: Baker, Benton, Clackamas, Clatsop, Columbia, Coos, Crook, Curry, Deschutes, Douglas, Gilliam, Grant, Harney, Hood River, Jackson, Jefferson, Josephine, Klamath, Lake, Lane, Lincoln, Linn, Malheur, Marion, Morrow, Multnomah, Polk, Sherman, Tillamook, Umatilla, Union, Wallowa, Wasco, Washington, Wheeler, Yamhill

Cities with population of 10,000 or more (1970 census): Albany, Ashland, Astoria, Beaverton, Bend, Coos Bay, Corvallis, Eugene, Grants Pass, Hillsboro, Klamath Falls, Lake Oswego, Medford, Milwaukie, Pendleton, Portland, Roseburg, Salem, Springfield

Elevation: Sea level to 11,245 feet (Mt. Hood)

Major industries: Lumbering, agriculture

First provisional government: 1843

Territorial status: 1848

Territorial motto: "Alis Volat Propriis" (She Flies With Her Own Wings)

Statehood: 1859

State motto: "The Union"

State colors: Navy blue and gold

State tree: Douglas fir

State fish: Chinook salmon

State rock: Thunдеregg

State bird: Western meadowlark

State flower: Oregon grape

SELECTED BIBLIOGRAPHY

American Guide Series; **OREGON**; Binfords & Mort; 1940.
ANNUAL REPORT; Keep Oregon Green Association, Inc.; 1964.
Bakeless, John; **THE ADVENTURES OF LEWIS & CLARK**; Houghton Mifflin; 1962.
Bakeless, John; **LEWIS & CLARK**; Morrow; 1947.
Beal, Merrill D.; **"I WILL FIGHT NO MORE FOREVER"**; U. of Washington; 1963.
Bidwell, John, Bancroft, Hubert Howe, and Longmire, James; **FIRST THREE WAGON TRAINS**; Binfords & Mort.
Blankenship, Russell; **AND THERE WERE MEN**; Knopf; 1942.
Brogan, Phil F.; **EAST OF THE CASCADES**; Binfords & Mort; 1964.
Brown, Mark H., and Felton, W. R.; **BEFORE BARBED WIRE**; Bramhall House; 1956.
Brown, Mark H., and Felton, W. R.; **THE FRONTIER YEARS**; Bramhall House; 1955.
Case, Robert Ormond; **THE EMPIRE BUILDERS**; Binfords & Mort; 1949.
Corbett-Atterbury, Vivian; **THE OREGON STORY**; Binfords & Mort; 1959.
Corning, Howard McKinley (ed.); **DICTIONARY OF OREGON HISTORY**; Binfords & Mort; 1956.
De Voto, Bernard; **THE JOURNALS OF LEWIS & CLARK**; Houghton Mifflin; 1953.
THE DOPE BUCKET; Spokane, Portland and Seattle Railroad; 1961.
Douthit, Mary Osborn; **THE SOUVENIR OF WESTERN WOMEN**; Anderson & Duniway; 1905.
Duniway, Abigail Scott; **PATH BREAKING**; 1914.
Dye, Eva Emery; **MCLOUGHLIN AND OLD OREGON**; Binfords & Mort; 1936.
EXPLORE FRONTIER JACKSONVILLE OREGON; Jackson County Chamber of Commerce; 1958.
Forbes, Robert H.; **"Here Comes 'Skyhook Logging!';"** **AMERICAN FORESTS**; January, 1965.
FORESTRY IN OREGON; Biennial Report of the State Forester, 1962-1964.
Freeman, Otis W., and Martin, Howard H. (eds.); **THE PACIFIC NORTHWEST**; Wiley; 1954.
French, Giles; **CATTLE COUNTRY OF PETER FRENCH**; Binfords & Mort; 1964.
Gibbs, James A., Jr.; **PACIFIC GRAVEYARD**; Binfords & Mort; 1950.
Gibbs, James A., Jr.; **SHIPWRECKS OF THE PACIFIC COAST**; Binfords & Mort; 1957.
Haines, Francis; **THE NEZ PERCES**; U. of Oklahoma; 1955.
Haines, Francis; **RED EAGLES OF THE NORTHWEST**; Scholastic; 1939.
Haines, Francis D., Jr., and Smith, Vern S.; **GOLD ON STERLING CREEK**; 1964.
Holbrook, Stewart H.; **THE AGE OF THE MOGULS**; Doubleday; 1953.
Holbrook, Stewart H.; **BURNING AN EMPIRE**; Macmillan; 1943.
Holbrook, Stewart H.; **JAMES J. HILL**; Knopf; 1955.
Holbrook, Stewart H.; **THE STORY OF AMERICAN RAILROADS**; Crown; 1947.
Hornung, Clarence P.; **WHEELS ACROSS AMERICA**; Barnes; 1959.
Howard, Helen Addison; **NORTHWEST TRAIL BLAZERS**; Caxton; 1963.
Howard, Helen Addison, and McGrath, Dan L.; **WAR CHIEF JOSEPH**; Caxton; 1958.
Johnson, Jalmar; **BUILDERS OF THE NORTHWEST**; Dodd, Mead; 1963.
Josephy, Alvin M., Jr.; **THE PATRIOT CHIEFS**; Viking; 1961.

THE JOURNALS OF CAPTAIN MERIWETHER LEWIS & SERGEANT JOHN
ORDWAY; Wisconsin State Historical Society; 1916.

Lavender, David; **LAND OF GIANTS**; Doubleday; 1958.

Lockley, Fred; **HISTORY OF THE COLUMBIA RIVER VALLEY FROM THE
DALLES TO THE SEA**; Clarke; 1928.

Lockley, Fred; **OREGON TRAIL BLAZERS**; Knickerbocker; 1929.

Maddux, Percy; **CITY ON THE WILLAMETTE**; Binfords & Mort; 1952.

Marquis, Albert Nelson (ed.); **WHO'S WHO IN AMERICA**; Marquis; 1940.

Meacham, Walter; **BARLOW ROAD**; 1947.

Meyers, E. L.; **A STORY OF TWO MEN FROM FORT DEPOSIT**; 1957 (mimeo-
graphed).

Mills, Randall V.; **STERNWHEELERS UP COLUMBIA**; Pacific Books; 1947.

Moody, John; **THE RAILROAD BUILDERS**; Yale University; 1919.

Moritz, Charles (ed.); **CURRENT BIOGRAPHY YEARBOOK**; Wilson; 1949, 1956,
1961.

NATURAL RESOURCES OF OREGON; U. S. Dept. of Interior; 1964.

Neuberger, Richard L.; **THE LEWIS & CLARK EXPEDITION**; Random; 1951.

Oliver, Herman; **GOLD AND CATTLE COUNTRY**; Binfords & Mort; 1961.

OREGON A TIMBER STATE; Oregon State Forestry Dept.; 1962.

OREGON HISTORIC LANDMARKS; Oregon Society, DAR; 1957.

OREGON HISTORICAL QUARTERLY; Oregon Historical Society (various issues).

OREGON 1965-1966 BLUE BOOK; Secretary of State; 1965.

Parrish, Philip H.; **HISTORIC OREGON**; Macmillan; 1949.

Payne, Doris Palmer; **CAPTAIN JACK, MODOC RENEGADE**; Binfords & Mort;
1938.

PHYSICAL AND ECONOMIC GEOGRAPHY OF OREGON; Oregon State Board
of Higher Education; 1940.

Port of Portland; various publications.

Quiett, Glenn Chesney; **THEY BUILT THE WEST**; Appleton-Century; 1934.

Rawling, Gerald; **THE PATHFINDERS**; Macmillan; 1964.

Riddle, George W.; **EARLY DAYS IN OREGON**; 1953.

Ross, Nancy Wilson; **WESTWARD THE WOMEN**; Random; 1944.

Salisbury, Albert and Jane; **HERE ROLLED THE COVERED WAGONS**;
Superior; 1948.

SCHOOL FOREST CONSERVATION TOURS IN OREGON; Oregon State University; 1964.

Scott, Harvey W.; **HISTORY OF THE OREGON COUNTRY**; Riverside; 1924.

Steffens, Joseph Lincoln; **UPBUILDERS**; Doubleday; 1909.

Sutton, Jack; **THE MYTHICAL STATE OF JEFFERSON**; Josephine County
Historical Society; 1965.

Sutton, Jack; **PICTORIAL HISTORY OF SOUTHERN OREGON AND NORTHERN
CALIFORNIA**; 1959.

Sutton, Jack, and Pinkham, Lee; **THE GOLDEN YEARS OF JACKSONVILLE**; 1961.

Talkington, Henry L.; **HEROES AND HEROIC DEEDS OF THE PACIFIC NORTH-
WEST**; Caxton; 1929.

Thwaites, Reuben Gold; **EARLY WESTERN TRAVELS**; Clark; 1906.

Van Every, Dale; **THE FINAL CHALLENGE**; Morrow; 1964.

Villard, Henry; **THE EARLY HISTORY OF TRANSPORTATION IN OREGON**;
U. of Oregon; 1944.

Walling, A. G.; **HISTORY OF SOUTHERN OREGON**; Walling; 1884.

WESTWARD ON THE OREGON TRAIL; American Heritage; 1962.

Wilson, Neill C., and Taylor, Frank J.; **SOUTHERN PACIFIC**; McGraw-Hill; 1951.

INDEX TO PERSONS AND PLACES

199

201